Parents and Children in the Hospital
The Family's Role in Pediatrics

Parents and Children in the Hospital

The Family's Role in Pediatrics

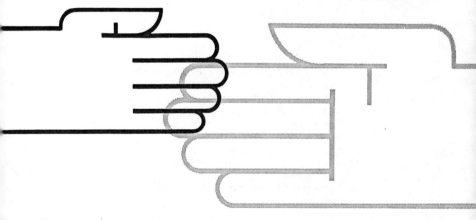

Carol B. Hardgrove, M.A.
Assistant Clinical Professor of Maternal Child Nursing
University of California School of Nursing
San Francisco

Rosemary B. Dawson

Little, Brown and Company, Boston

Library of Congress catalog card No. 74-187709
First Edition
ISBN 0-316-34600
*Published in Great Britain by Churchill/Livingstone,
Edinburgh and London*
Printed in the United States of America

Cover design by Richard Emery

Preface

DURING the last three decades, an increasing body of research has indicated the importance of meeting the emotional and developmental needs of young children during times of hospitalization. As long ago as the 1940's, Sir James Spence in England made a practice of admitting mothers to the hospital along with toddlers and infants. The classic studies of maternal deprivation made by Dr. John Bowlby for the World Health Organization and published in 1951 have documented beyond question the tragic and far-reaching effects on young children of being deprived of the ongoing warmth and care of a mother or mother substitute. Work done by Erik Erikson, Anna Freud, Dane Prugh, René Spitz, and others has confirmed and underlined the necessity of further understanding the needs of children in times of stress and of meeting those needs realistically.

Today there is still ample evidence that, while many children in American hospitals receive high-quality technical care, their social and emotional development may be permanently damaged because little attention is paid to their reactions to separation from the family. In 1968, only 28 of

5,000 general hospitals had facilities allowing parents to spend the night with their child; of 132 children's hospitals only 20 allowed rooming-in, and of these, 15 admitted only mothers from upper socioeconomic groups.[1] The figures are little improved today.

Aware of the growing concern of many professional people with the total development of the hospitalized child, we undertook this study because of our interest in the well-being of preschool children in particular, mindful of our personal experience when our own children were in the hospital, and because our professional experience had indicated so clearly the need for more widespread understanding of children's reactions to hospitalization. Our intention was not to compile further statistics on the extent and kinds of impairment that can be caused in children, nor to tabulate the degrees and kinds of care given in all United States hospitals. Rather, we selected a sampling of hospitals currently carrying out new and innovative programs for meeting the needs of both the hospitalized child and his family. These programs are described in a way intended to show as accurately as possible what they are really like from day to day, what the tone of the units conveys to the family and the child, and what the professional staff says and feels about such programs.

Questionnaires, compiled with the help of the Association for Child Care in Hospitals, were sent to institutions which we knew had embarked on policies stressing the emotional and developmental health of children. From the responses to the questionnaires we selected a cross section of both large public institutions and smaller community or university

---

[1]Dombro, R. H. Mothers in the Hospital. Presented at the Conference of the American Association for Child Care in Hospitals, Cleveland, May, 1968.

hospitals that best illustrate the many ways in which the needs of children can be met and family participation in their care encouraged. Not all the hospitals are included that, at this writing, were breaking new ground in the area of family participation or were making efforts to change old policies. Many had moved toward more liberal visiting hours and were developing a more realistic awareness of the psychological factors involved in physical illness; to document all such policies and programs is beyond our scope. We have tried, instead, to demonstrate that new ways of insuring better care for children can be workable under a wide variety of conditions.

During our research we were constantly made aware of the negative response to change in many institutions; any suggestions about new approaches were countered with positive assurance that while liberalized policies might be feasible elsewhere, they would be unworkable in the particular hospital's situation or with its particular personnel. However, while resisting more liberal policies, most of these hospitals considered them desirable and were aware of children's need for more humanized and less mechanical care.

By describing programs that have translated knowledge into action, we hope that we can offer some ideas for dealing with barriers often cited as prohibitive. Some of the institutions we visited are old and limited by less than adequate space; some are public institutions serving large urban areas; others serve a scattered rural population. All, however, share one characteristic: they have inaugurated, within their individual limitations, programs that reach out to include the families of children under their care, and all are as much concerned with the emotional and developmental growth of their patients as they are with the curing of physical symptoms.

This study was made possible by Small Research Grant No. 17230-01 from the National Institute of Mental Health and by the cooperation of the University of California, San Francisco, School of Nursing. The opinions and evaluations expressed are our own; the limitations are also our own.

Helpful and generous cooperation was provided by the many hospitals that allowed us access to their programs and whose staff members gave us personal interviews. Finally, we are greatly indebted to the many doctors, nurses, social workers, child activities staff members, and parents and their children who answered our questions in wards, living-in units, hallways, and playrooms.

"I thought we'd been stockpiling shovels long enough," Dr. Joseph Butterfield said of research at his Newborn Center in The Children's Hospital, Denver, "so I decided to dig a hole." To all the dedicated professionals and parents who are digging that hole with the tools at hand, our admiration and our thanks.

C. B. H.
R. B. D.

Contents

Contents

Parents and Children in the Hospital
The Family's Role in Pediatrics

1

The Child, the Parent, and the Professionals

"THE aftermath of a lengthy stay in a hospital in the early years is commonly an extended period of serious maladaptation and unhappiness for the child and serious difficulties for the family to whose care he is returned. Even if, in the course of years, the child is one of those whose mental recovery is complete, the cost in terms of stress, family friction, and wasted months or years is high." So said James Robertson in 1958.[1]

"It is not surprising that nonpsychiatric physicians, especially pediatricians, nurses, and hospital administrators, failing to understand the relationship of early life experiences to emotional development and behavior, often have been unable to see the influence of their roles in child care in promoting mental health and illness," wrote Dr. Milton Senn.[2]

---

[1]Robertson, J. *Young Children in Hospital*. London, England: Travistock, 1958.

[2]Senn, M. Foreword. In M. F. Shore (Ed.), *Red Is the Color of Hurting*. Bethesda, Md.: National Institute of Mental Health, 1967.

"It is clear by now that all children from very early infancy show at least some temporary reactions to hospitalization itself insofar as this can be differentiated from their responses to the particular illness or operation. Such reactions, of course, take different forms at different age levels. These developmental issues are of major significance in viewing the effects of hospitalization," according to Dr. D. G. Prugh.[3]

John Bowlby, in his research, found "case histories of some dozens of children whose neurotic symptoms had either developed or been made worse by separation from the mother, most of the separation experiences being in hospital. In about half of them the experience of separation occurred during the first three years, in the other half between about three and eight years. In many of the latter the children could describe clearly how they had felt in hospital, common anxieties being the beliefs either that they would not return home, or that they were being sent away for being naughty."[4]

The above are some of the conclusions reached after studies made in this and other countries since the 1950's. The work of Anna Freud,[5] S. Wolf,[6] and E. H. Erikson[7] confirms these findings.

---

[3]Prugh, D. G. Emotional Aspects of the Hospitalized Child. In M. F. Shore (Ed.), *Red Is the Color of Hurting.* Bethesda, Md.: National Institute of Mental Health, 1967.

[4]Bowlby, J. *Child Care and the Growth of Love* (2nd ed.). Baltimore: Penguin Books, 1965.

[5]Freud, A. The role of bodily illness in the mental life of children. *Psychoanalytic Study of the Child* 7:69, 1952.

[6]Wolf, S. *Children under Stress.* New York: Penguin Press, 1969.

[7]Erikson, E. H. *Childhood and Society* (rev. ed.). New York: W. W. Norton, 1968.

OBSERVATIONS MADE ON PEDIATRIC UNITS

Case Histories

Some notes taken on a pediatric unit by a child-activities specialist:

A big boy, 4 1/2 years old, had a net over his bed, and there was evidence of diapers having been used as ties.

The boy asked, "Nurse—nurse—nurse—can I go to the playroom?"

"No. You cannot. And stop asking," the nurse replied.

"Why not?"

"You know why not. I gave you plenty of warning."

In answer to my questions, the nurse said that the boy was being punished because he swore, bit, spat, and threw charts on the floor.

I talked to him, and we played puppets. He reacted joyously and appropriately, responding readily to questions. I brought him some cars and trucks from the playroom.

In the elevator later, I saw him being carried by his big, jolly father. He looked very happy. I said, "Hey, you got out!" and he grinned at me. His pretty, dark-haired mother said, "He's been such a wonderful boy!" I decided not to tell.

A red-haired, 2-year-old girl whimpered steadily as the nurse bathed her. She cried softly. The nurse said, "Stop crying. You know what will happen if you keep crying? You'll use all your tears up, and then some day when you need them you won't have any." This to a 2-year-old!

An adult, recalling a childhood hospitalization:

My mouth was so sore and I couldn't eat. A dietician or somebody brought in a tray and told me to eat it all up or I couldn't get well and go home. She left, and I took the big hamburger off the tray and threw it out the window—I was on the ground floor. I looked out to see where it had landed, and it was lying in a whitewashed sort of area, way below the window. My heart was just pounding, and I got back in bed and tried to eat everything else, but I was so afraid that the nurse or someone would look out and see it. I was afraid of what they would do to me. But the next day, luckily, I went home. I don't know if anyone found it.

An observation made in a pediatric unit by a specialist in early childhood education:

J., 6 1/2 months old, was alone in a crib in a room. She was immobilized because her legs were tied down—one had an intravenous tube (I.V.) going in. The I.V. went dry before the nurse came to check. The nurse brought in and mounted a mobile—an activator and a couple of plastic toys, well selected for this child's age. J. cried loudly, vigorously, and unceasingly.

There was a bottle of apple juice on the table behind her, but the nurse told me that while I could try if I cared to, J. had refused all liquids for the three days she had been hospitalized.

I stayed with her for forty-five minutes; after I had been in the room for ten minutes, J. stopped crying for minutes at a time, and when I handed her the plastic toys, she examined them attentively. After half an hour, I again tried to give her the bottle of apple juice; she drank all but an ounce, and then cried and refused more.

She had spunk enough to keep protesting. I know it takes twenty to thirty minutes before a child exhibits any behavior that is faithful to his real self; seldom did anyone on the unit devote half an hour to this. There was a bed in the room that the mother could have used. Had she been told that she could? The nurse didn't know. I checked the chart and found that the father was away; the mother lived with relatives in the city, and there was a grandmother nearby. Clearly, the mother, if informed that her child was suffering without her and that there was a place nearby where she could sleep, could have prevented a great deal of distress in this baby. Would the child have accepted fluids from the mother, and would the I.V. have been necessary if the child were taking fluids? Couldn't the mother have been taught to monitor the I.V. and inform the nurse when it ran out? Weren't we unnecessarily damaging this child?

The incidents related above concerning children on pediatric units are not isolated examples, nor are they extreme; none of the children were terminally ill nor in an acute crisis situation. They are examples of the lack of communication and awareness that arises when there is no policy of treating the child as an individual person. The 4 1/2-year-old boy was perceived by his parents as a child who had coped well with a strange situation; by the early childhood education specialist he was seen as a child who was active and outgoing and who needed to be helped to handle his own rebellion against the situation of restraint and loneliness in which he found himself; and by the nurse he was regarded as a child who failed to conform and was a troublemaker who deserved punishment.

To the 2-year-old girl, the world was entirely a place of despair. Her steady crying, alone or when an adult was attending her, was a total and hopeless protest against her condition. The nurse perceived her as someone who could stop crying if she wanted to and who could be coaxed—or perhaps frightened a little at the thought of tears drying up—by a conversation that an older child would comprehend but that a 2-year-old would understand imperfectly, if at all.

The child who threw her hamburger out the window saw

the dietician as a strange, avenging force who would tell punitive authorities of any transgression. The dietician saw only a little girl who was given a nice lunch and should be encouraged to eat it.

J., who at 6 months could only communicate her rage with loud and steady protesting cries, was perceived by the nurse as a child who was being given good care and suitable toys and who cried because children do cry in the hospital. The observer saw her as an infant in shock as a result of restraint and maternal separation and who might have taken liquids normally if her mother had been there, thus avoiding undue restraint and perhaps intravenous feeding. The mother's opinion and perceptions of her child and the possible support that she could have given were not solicited, and therefore it is not possible to tell whether the child's situation would have been entirely different if the mother had been present.

It is, of course, not possible to tell to what degree these children were harmed and to what degree they may have regressed in development, both physically and emotionally, because of the ways in which they perceived the hospital situation. That they could have been harmed and that many of their feelings of panic, rage, loneliness, and rebellion could have been allayed is made abundantly clear by research.

PARENTS IN THE HOSPITAL

It would be an oversimplification to assume that the physical presence of the parent, either living in with the child or spending long daytime hours by the bedside, would automatically have mitigated some of the distress these children showed. There is some justification for the feeling of hospital personnel that parents can be a problem and a burden to an already busy staff. When the question of admitting the parents to partnership in the care of a child arises, an assumption is sometimes made by staff and administration that this means admitting all parents, with no guidelines concerning their role, and with the nurses required to assume the burden of the child's total care while fending off, or evading, the troublesome demands and needs of parents.

As we shall see, hospitals which have successfully made use of the parents' skills are under no such illusions. They are well aware that the policy cannot be "business as usual" with an influx of parents unfamiliar with the hospital routine and with the child's needs. On the contrary, they realize that parents must be prepared, educated, and supported in helping their children. To do this the staff must be aware of the positive benefits to the child, who is, after all, the first concern of a pediatric unit. They must be aware, as well, of the benefits to the staff when parents can contribute in a positive way. Unless the administration and medical staff of a hospital are convinced of the necessity of meeting a child's emotional and developmental as well as physical needs, a nurse is often in a position of being torn between the carrying out of rigid policy and the importunities of parents.

The pressure of responsibility, the lack of time to do all that needs to be done, the difficulty of assuming authority at the same time that one is accountable to a higher authority, all can make for a stressful situation for a nurse, one that is compounded in times of crisis and emergency. It is thus not surprising that parents are often seen as one more problem in a complicated schedule and that their questions, their fears, and their very physical presence are interpreted as an additional, unnecessary burden on the nursing staff. To avoid such problems, rules are useful—"It's hospital policy. Those are the rules." Such absolutes are a safeguard for the nurse when difficult situations arise, saving time, individual decisions, and personal involvement.

One common element observable in most hospitals in which the policy is one of excluding parents is the reiteration of generalizations about them. Most frequently voiced is: "The children behave much better when their parents aren't here. We don't have any trouble until they show up, and the children quiet right down as soon as the parents go away." This generalization, including as it does all parents, all age levels of patients, and all degrees of illness in one blanket statement, covers many debatable assumptions. It assumes, for instance, that all showing of emotion by a child when the parent appears is undesirable, whereas the very display of rage or sadness by the child may be an indication of a healthy rebellion rather than apathy. It further assumes that children are happy in the hospital except when a family member is present. As observation of any pediatric unit shows and as the previously cited episodes demonstrate, children do not settle down and cheerfully accept pain and loneliness simply because their mothers are not with them. The crying of children seems open to interpretation in at least two ways: a child crying alone (e.g., J.) is seen by the nurse as simply a crying child, a natural enough phenomenon in a hospital. A crying child whose mother has just arrived, however, is seen as a child whose mother is upsetting him unnecessarily by her presence and who would probably be happier if she were not there.

Another common generalization is that parents are content to leave their children in the care of experts, that they are relieved to be free of responsibility, and that they would be made to feel too guilty or inadequate if any suggestion were put forward that they be present. This is true only of some parents, and then only in varying degrees. Of other parents it is entirely untrue. More importantly, this generalization omits the need to find out why some parents feel this way (if indeed they do), what can be done to make a healthier relationship within the family with reassurance for both child and parent, and whether the hospital has an obligation to contribute to the developmental and emotional health of the child within the context of his family in addition to curing his physical ills. It also takes for granted that there is no need to ask parents what they feel; it assumes there is a standardized group under the label "parents." This is the more surprising since any good hospital would resist such labels in its own specialties: to categorize all fractures of any kind under a general label of "broken bones" without any further investigation would be entirely contrary to medical or nursing standards. "Parents" are really individual persons. In order to get some idea of what their feelings really are, let us see what some parents have to say about the ways in which they have interpreted their interactions with doctors, nurses, and hospitals.

RELATIONSHIPS BETWEEN PARENTS AND HOSPITAL STAFF

The baby was 9 months old when he got sick. We called the doctor, who told us to give him orange juice and glucose. We all thought it was just the flu. By the next morning he was so much sicker that we called the doctor very early. He saw the baby at noon and rushed him to the hospital in an ambulance. I went with the baby. The ambulance man didn't talk much. Once he said, "Is he still breathing?" and that really scared me. When we got to the emergency unit, they took the baby away—but I stood right outside the door where they had taken him. Nurses and doctors came in and out but nobody spoke to me or looked at me. I didn't know what was happening. They had told me to wait, so I just waited. After about forty-five minutes an intern or somebody came—I didn't know him. He said, "Are you the mother?" I guess he didn't know who I was. Then he said, "The baby could have died." He sounded as if it was my fault. Then he told me that the baby was going to be all right, and that they were going to take him to the Intensive Care Unit and I could go with him. Pretty soon a nurse came out with the baby and I went upstairs with them. When I asked, she told me where they were taking him and that I had to wait to see the doctor. I guess I couldn't believe what was happening, and I didn't even know what to say. The nurse didn't talk to me, but when we got there she told me I could call the hospital any time to find out how he was.

They put him in a room with about ten children. There was a glass window you could look through. I called my husband and waited. He came right away, and after a while the doctor came and took us into a room and asked us a lot of questions. He made us feel that we had done something wrong—that it was all our fault that the baby had gotten sick. They were just questions, but they gave you that feeling. He filled out a blank form and kept asking questions. Finally I said, "Why are you being like this to us? Why are you making us think that we're bad parents? Do you think we don't love our baby?" Then he told us that there are so many cases of child neglect and child battering that they have to ask all those questions. But why did he treat us as if we were that kind of parents? We aren't.

After that, the baby was there for about three days. We couldn't be with him, and when we went to see him we could only look at him through the glass. Every time he saw us he cried so hard that we thought it was bad for him; the nurse said that seeing us upset him, so after that we didn't go to see him.

When they gave him to me to take home, he cried and clung to me like a little monkey—he gripped so hard that I couldn't put him down even for a minute. It was the same at home—for the next few days I carried him everywhere—I didn't do anything else but take care of him. When we put him to bed at night we had to hold him until he was really deeply asleep. Then we'd slide him into his crib, and if he woke up he would scream in an awful panic—I never heard him make that sound before or after. It wasn't a cry or anything, it was an awful scream. That's why I had him with me all the time—he was only quiet if he was with one of us. It gradually wore off, but for those days I didn't do anything at all but take care of him; I put a chair right by his bed so that if he woke at night and screamed, I could hold him.

It's like a factory in that hospital. You come in and they never know who you are. They did say I could call them, and one of the nurses who answered the telephone would say my name. The others didn't. Nobody told us anything about the visiting hours or if there was anywhere we could wait. I never even thought that we could have been near him—it was just set up so that we knew we weren't supposed to be around. Nobody told me that after we took him home he might be like that. Luckily, we could call the doctor—I did call him a lot after we had the baby at home again and he was acting so strangely—and he would reassure me.

If I had been alone with nobody to talk to, or if my husband had been less sympathetic and helpful, I don't know what I would have done. Nobody told us of any way that we could help, or what to expect, or what to do. Starting with the ambulance driver, who asked me if the baby was still breathing, and then the man—a resident or an intern, I imagine; he didn't say who he was—who asked if I was the mother and said the baby could have died, and then the doctor who asked all those questions in a way that made us feel that we had done everything wrong and had neglected the baby, and all the rest of the people who never looked at you or said anything, as if you weren't even there at all—all of it was like a factory in a nightmare. Even when they gave us the baby to take home, nobody said anything. They just handed him over. But that one nurse who sometimes answered the telephone was nice. She knew my name, and she used it when she talked to me.

That was the experience of one college-educated, loving, and intelligent mother with a children's hospital of excellent reputation in a major city. She was fortunate in having a private physician who admitted the baby to the hospital and in having the leisure that made it possible for her to devote most of her time to the baby for the week following his release, helping him recover from the shock of illness and separation. When asked what she would have done if she had been a working mother who had to leave him, if she had been the mother of many children who also needed attention, or if she had been a non-English-speaking mother, she said that it was impossible to imagine what she would have done. "I really couldn't put him down for the first day or so after he came home; he clung to me so tightly and was in such a panic if I left him. It wasn't that he was spoiled, or naughty—he was only 9 months old and he was like someone out of his mind."

The hospital had saved this baby's life in a crisis, but the way in which the care was perceived by both baby and mother made for maximum emotional stress for both. Was this unavoidable, given the urgency of the situation and the need for immediate treatment?

A nurse told of a friend whose toddler was hospitalized.

She came to me and said that her baby was dead. She said that he was in a mist tent and nobody would let her go in, nobody would say anything about him, and she couldn't hear or see him. She was sure that he had died and that they were waiting for the doctor to tell her. I went with her and took her into the room, and she could see that he was sleeping easily. Then she calmed down.

This mother saw the hospital as a place of frightening secrecy and felt shut out of the conspiracy which she felt surrounded her own child. At the same time she may have been perceived by the nursing staff as an obstacle to the child's care, standing outside the door, asking unnecessary questions, getting in the way.

At a smaller, well-staffed community hospital which makes a policy of involving parents in the care of their children, one mother indignantly told this story.

My little boy is only 2 years old. He isn't on a restricted diet, but his lunch didn't come. I heard the trays come up and go away again. After a while a nurse made rounds and said to him, "Did you have a nice lunch?" She just asked it in a chatty sort of way. When I told her that he hadn't had anything at all, she didn't believe me. She said that he must have, because all the trays had come and gone. But she went to find out, and sure enough I was right. They then brought him something. But what I want to know is—what would have happened if I hadn't been there? He's only 2, and he doesn't talk very plainly. She wouldn't have believed him, or he wouldn't have told her. Then if he'd been hungry and cried, they would have thought he was a naughty boy.

This mother, as many do, saw the hospital as a place where the child will be forgotten or neglected except for medical care unless someone is there to protect him. Whether or not she had any basis for this belief, it influenced her trust in the hospital staff and her willingness to accept their authority over the child's well-being and may have communicated to the child himself feelings which made nursing him more difficult.

The grandmother of a hospitalized child voiced much the same attitude.

My daughter doesn't leave him. Poor thing, I'm afraid she's going to drop. I have to bring her a sandwich. She comes early in the morning and stays until he goes to sleep at night. They're so understaffed here . . . If it weren't for her, he'd just have to lie in his bed and cry. They don't have time to do any more than give him his treatments and feed him. Poor baby.

This was less a criticism of the staff than a resigned acceptance of what she considered inevitable—the impersonality of an institution. It was, in fact, somewhat the same kind of attitude often held toward computers: at the mercy of the inexorable working of the machine, one can only defend oneself as well as possible and put up with the inconvenience.

One mother spoke of her young daughter's tonsillectomy.

We stood there in the hall and watched them take the children up to surgery. They had three of them strapped down to one wheeled table, and they had given them something that dried up the fluids so that they didn't cry tears. They were all strapped down together—my little girl and two others—and they were squealing with fear like little pigs. I couldn't do anything—I had nightmares about it for months. I don't want to think about it.

Several years had passed since that episode, but still the mother remembered it with horror.

To hear similar stories one has only to ask any group of parents how they felt when a child was hospitalized. A characteristic feature of the parents' description of hospitalization is the tendency to blame themselves for not having protected the child or for having left him by himself to face a strange and frightening experience.

"They told me that he acted up when I came and behaved better when I wasn't there," a mother will say apologetically, "so I didn't visit often." The tone is hesitant, most mothers saying that it was hard to leave, that they couldn't bear to hear the child call out for them. They were torn between the child's obvious distress and need for them and the authority which told them that they were doing harm to the child they loved. Some parents express a hope that the child will be "good" in the hospital, as though he could placate those who might victimize him when the parents are helpless to stand between him and authority. That the child might be in pain or sedated, less equipped than at any other time to take his destiny into his own hands, too young to communicate adequately, all somehow become less realistic than the hope that by being good he can survive an experience which is frightening even to adults. Perhaps if he is good they will not need to know what he experienced; perhaps it will all be forgotten because "he's too young to remember; children forget things so fast."

The stories of these parents typify some of the ways in which many families view the hospitalization of their children. They turn to the hospital in times of stress because they must; they trust the medical judgment of the doctors and nurses, but they rarely expect that their feelings of concern for their children will be respected. Even more rarely does it occur to them that they could have a positive and supportive role to play in the child's recovery. The rising costs of hospitalization can add to their feeling that they and the children are in some way being victimized even while they are being helped.

Parents at this time are under unusual stresses, ranging from a feeling of guilt for having been in some way responsible for the child's illness to fears of what he will undergo and lack of knowledge about the illness and the treatment. Financial worries, the fear that the child will die, and worry that the child will reject the parents are often involved as well. Sometimes marital problems are intensified by a child's illness. Conflicts of responsibility between being at home and being with the child are often unresolved. There is also sometimes resentment of the burden of coping with the illness and, by extension, of the child himself. These stresses and uncertainties all play a part in the different ways in which parents see and react to the professionals who care for their child, and they influence the child himself and his hospital experience.

The professional staff also bring certain predispositions and attitudes to their relationships and interactions with the parents. The belief that parents get in the way was succinctly stated by a head nurse in a well-endowed community hospital: "They bring the children here because they know that we will give them the best of care. Why should the parents be here themselves? There's no reason for them to pay for good care and then have to come in. It's our job." The assumption here was that the hospital did not need any contribution that the parents could make, that mothering as well as medical care could be supplied better and more efficiently by the staff than by the parents.

The nurse, skilled and trained in her profession, is an authority in a pediatric unit. It cannot be otherwise, since she has not only the expertise but the responsibility for seeing that treatment is carried out, keeping records, making judgments (often several times in an hour), and handling many patients and many kinds of equipment. She cannot leave her feelings behind when she enters the unit: some children appeal to her more than others for special reasons, some doctors appear to respect her less than others, and some families arrive at a busy time or during a time of crisis. Throughout her crowded day, despite outside and inner pressures, she must still keep in mind that she is an authority and that she must be the judge in many cases of what is best for the child and his family.

At the same time the parents are also authorities, particularly the mother, who is most often the parent with the closest relationship with the child and the one who is most likely to stay with him. At home she is the central figure, and the child's attitudes, nutrition, habits, and way of life depend on her. Her love and care, her affection or withholding of it, and her attitudes toward the world around the family are basic conditions of the child's growth and development. She is suddenly faced with a usurping of her role; often she cannot help but feel that this situation is arbitrary, unfeeling, and frightening. She knows that her child would be quieter and more amenable to treatment if he could have his familiar toy, if he could hold her hand, if she could talk to him in the familiar language of home. She, as well as the child, is often stunned and angry at what appears to be a callous separation. She is shut out, a prey to fears of what may happen, and perhaps she also reacts to past memories and fears of the unfamiliar figures in white with whom she has had painful or frightening experiences. She can often translate the child's language when others misunderstand him; she hears him calling out to her or crying, and all her authority as his mother, all the past love and care she has given him, dictate that she brush aside these strangers and protect and help him.

The mother can easily look upon the nurse as an arbitrary and hostile stranger. The doctor, in his special role of authority with the weight of position and knowledge, whom she sees less often and more impersonally, must be trusted. The child is in a precarious position, and someone must be trusted—faith therefore can be placed in the omnipotent doctor. The nurse, however, is seen many times, lives in this unfamiliar world, and seems to be displacing the mother by easing the child's pain and caring for him in a way that the mother cannot. On the other hand, she may be causing him pain in a way that the mother interprets as callous and unfeeling; she brushes aside the mother's questions, apparently not interested in the family's feelings, carrying out a set routine and ritual in which there is no place for human emotion or personal contact. At such times the nurse may be entirely unaware of the reactions engendered in the mother and the child; the mother may be equally unaware that there is a shortage of staff on that particular day, or that a crisis has arisen on the unit, or that the nurse has worked long hours and her relief is already overdue.

Speaking of relationships between parents and nurses which can develop into distrust, mutual criticism, and defensiveness, Sir James Spence pointed out, "A common way out of this dilemma is for parents and nurses to have as little to do with each other as possible."[8] This lack of communication is sometimes demonstrated at group meetings of parents during which criticism or questions are not voiced when staff members are present, although the staff may be there for the very purpose of communicating and is making

---

[8]Spence, J. The Care of Children in Hospital. In *The Purpose and Practice of Medicine*. New York: Oxford University Press, 1960.

every effort to be open and to encourage comment. As soon as several parents are assured that they will not be overheard by the staff, however—perhaps when they break up into small groups at the end of the same meeting—there may be bitter criticism of the staff with a tendency to overstress trifles or to express disproportionate indignation with the routine or personnel.

When close contact on a unit is accompanied by a great gulf in awareness and communication, misunderstandings can grow into serious problems. One resident in a large hospital, coming rapidly through the pediatric unit, greeted a 3-year-old boy who had a disproportionately swollen abdomen with, "Hello there, Humpty-Dumpty! How are you today?" and a cheerful laugh. He then disappeared through the door, unconscious of the indignation behind him and of the feelings of the child, whose hearing was normal and who was well aware that he had been made the butt of an unkind adult joke. It is possible that the resident thought of himself as "having a way with children." It is also possible that in any future contact with that particular child, the resident would be surprised to find the child turn from him and show dislike or fear, or to have the parents less than cooperative. Such episodes, trivial as they are when they occur, may be added to bit by bit until the entire treatment of a child is made more difficult and the child himself carries a burden of resentment and insecurity which could easily have been prevented.

If such misunderstanding and poor communication exist, as they do in many hospitals, the solution "to have as little to do with each other as possible" seems to be effective. Limited visiting hours, circumscribed areas in which parents are allowed, and strict adherence to the rules, backed by authority, can keep parents from interfering with routine and can keep children relatively quiet and obedient. It is thus not surprising that many institutions find it easier to carry out such policies, in so doing ignoring the obvious fact that hospitals were founded in order to better the health of patients, not to add emotional trauma and developmental retardation to the physical disabilities that brought them there for medical care.

RESISTANCE TO CHANGE

One reason put forward by many hospital administrations and staffs to explain their reluctance to take seriously the research done in the fields of child development and child psychiatry is that, with the technological advances made in medicine and surgery, hospitals have become instruments for training and research in which patients supply the necessary material for teaching medical students and for testing advances in various specialties. The patients, to be sure, are cared for, but their total well-being is secondary to the needs of the doctors, whose interests lie in areas not concerned with individuals. Many hospitals have financial commitments to new and sophisticated equipment; many are teaching institutions that are linked with colleges and universities; many have staffs with such specialized interests that, in the words of one concerned and thoughtful doctor, "our children are subject to fractured care here—moved from place to place arbitrarily for the convenience of the subspecialists. Nobody thinks of the child as a person and is concerned with what is happening to him and how he feels about it all."

Another reason given for resistance to change is the complexity and size of hospitals and a predisposition on the part of some administrators and staff to consider any change a threat to the functioning of the organization. The administration in one children's hospital with excellent facilities and equipment appeared to welcome the possibility of including parents and talked enthusiastically of a new policy, but they have failed to implement it. The reason given for this was: "We ought to have beds for parents in more than one small unit. It ought to be hospital policy that parents can stay in all of our units. We don't have the funding or facilities right now, so we really should wait until we can do it properly. People might criticize us if we had only a few living-in beds; perhaps when we expand our facilities in a year or two we can plan for parents to be here." The architect's drawings for this expansion are already completed, and there are no provisions for including parents. In this hospital parents may stay only upon request of their doctor and only in extreme cases, whereas in several older hospitals with far less adequate space for families, the policy of parents participating in their children's care has been in force for several years.

It seems obvious that some administrations, while well acquainted with the findings on children's emotional needs, consider them relatively unimportant. Dr. John Bowlby in his classic work on maternal deprivation[9] suggested another reason for failure to implement new policies:

The dramatic and tragic changes in behavior and feeling which follow separation of the young child from his mother and the beneficent results of restoring him to her are in fact available for all to see, and it is astonishing that so little attention has been given to them hitherto. So painful, indeed, are the agonies which these children suffer on separation that it may well be that those who have their care shut their eyes

---

[9]Bowlby, J. *Maternal Care and Mental Health.* New York: Schocken Books, 1966.

in self-protection. Yet of their existence there can be no doubt, as distressingly similar pictures are given by numerous different investigators.

In hospitals with admirable physical facilities and excellent modern equipment and in which research, training, and teaching are stressed, it may well be easier to "shut their eyes in self-protection," since to restudy hospital care in terms of human needs and to look upon children as individuals may mean a far-reaching change in emphasis and policy. Such changes are by no means easy to achieve. Those in administrative positions may look upon changes as a threat; the smooth-running routine of a unit may be upset by the very presence of outsiders; those who depend for their own self-esteem on the exercise of authority often may greatly resist having to temper that authority or share it. Groups with particular expertise in any field tend to guard against encroachment by strangers from outside who are not knowledgeable in their specialty. Boards of directors, scientists in particular specialties, and faculties of educational institutions may find pressures to change or demands for a new direction very nearly intolerable.

An extremely knowledgeable physician, who has succeeded in initiating many changes, has found that: "You can't ask whether or not there should be a change in any given unit. Normally, the human reaction is to resist change. When I want to try even a small innovation, I take responsibility for the change, assume that it is decided upon, and enlist the help of the staff as to how it can best be done. Once they become interested in the problem and are able to put their own ideas about it into effect, it usually is very successful." The pediatric section in this hospital is notable for the many small ways in which the young patients and their parents are made to feel personally welcome and at home. Each change in policy here, large or small, is reached by asking the simple questions, "What would make people feel better? What would they like?"

An approach as straightforward as this, however, is often difficult to implement; even under optimal conditions the limitations of space, time, funds, staffing, and record-keeping can get in the way of change. Such difficulties, compounded by lack of understanding on the part of the administration and the hospital personnel, may mean that needed changes are postponed indefinitely.

Nevertheless, they do occur. Increasing awareness of how children can be victimized by hospitalization—even when the intention is kindness and good care—and of the positive advantages of enlisting the skills of parents and educating them to safeguard their children have resulted in far-reaching and beneficial changes in many institutions. The most cursory observation of the hospitals which have moved toward parent participation shows the range of imagination and innovation released when those in authority take seriously the emotional and developmental well-being of the child patient. The rewards for the nurses and the parents are easily demonstrable as well.

"I couldn't go back to working in the other kind of hospital again," is reiterated by nurses in many units of these hospitals.

"I just tell any nurses who question our policies how it was before the parents were allowed to be here," said a head nurse. "I have lots of horror stories."

"Sometimes we go down to the clinic just to visit one of the children we've cared for who is back for a checkup," nurses say.

"This was a unit for children who were immobilized in

bed. It was dull and isolated and had been going on in the same way for years," said one forward-looking and innovative pediatrician. "The head nurse was 70 years old, and she wasn't convinced it could be done any other way. But after we had talked for a while, started the classroom here, and opened things up and encouraged activity and dialogue with the families, she began to be really enthusiastic and interested. She just hadn't known it could be any other way. It was remarkable . . ."

"Anyone can make a beginning," say those who have done it.

"I just know that we like it better; the children like it better, and so do the parents," is frequently heard from doctors, nurses, and social workers.

"You're asking the wrong question," said Dr. Avrum Katcher of the Hunterdon Medical Center in New Jersey. "Your question should not be 'Who does it?' but 'Why is it taking so long?' There's been plenty of evidence; hospitals know about it—why aren't they all doing it?"

REFERENCES

Baty, J., and Tisza, V. B. The impact of illness on the child and his family. *Child Study* 34:15-19, 1956-1957.

Bowlby, J. The nature of the child's tie to his mother. *International Journal of Psychoanalysis* 39:350-373, 1958.

Dombro, R. The surgically ill child and his family. *Surgical Clinics of North America* 50:431, 1970.

Mason, E. A. The hospitalized child—his emotional needs. *New England Journal of Medicine* 272:406-414, 1965.

Provence, S., and Lipton, R. *Infants in Institutions.* New York: International Universities Press, 1967.

Rich, J. *Interviewing Children and Adolescents.* New York: Macmillan Co., 1968.

Robertson, J. *Hospitals and Children.* New York: International Universities Press, 1963.

Vernon, D. T. (Ed.), Foley, J. M., Sipowicz, R. R., and Schulman, J. L. *The Psychological Response of Children to Hospitalization and Illness.* Springfield, Ill.: C. C Thomas 1965.

2

Parents and Children
Come to Stay

THREE of the institutions studied in this survey have
facilities planned for the specific purpose of allowing family
members to live at the hospital and participate in the care of
their children: The Henrietta Egleston Hospital for Children
in Atlanta, Georgia, the University of Kentucky Medical
Center in Lexington, and Boston Floating Hospital for
Infants and Children. All three are teaching hospitals linked
to universities, all have research programs, and in all of them
rooms are provided in which a parent and child may stay
together. Henrietta Egleston Hospital and Boston Floating
Hospital treat only the acutely ill child; the University of
Kentucky Medical Center is a general hospital in which one
section, the Care-by-Parent Unit, carries out a special
program for parent involvement.

Although there are differences in geographic setting,
caseloads, available facilities, and operational details between
any two of them, all share certain noticeable similarities.
First, they are all convinced that children need close ties with
their families during times of stress and that there are positive

values to be gained by using a parent's presence to reassure and help the child. Second, they all express respect for the abilities of parents to learn techniques and nursing procedures and have expanded the traditional concept of nursing to include the role of educator. Third, the position of a nurse in these hospitals is generally that of a team member of the medical staff rather than a handmaiden to the physician as traditionally. Therefore, there is more communication among various disciplines, and ongoing plans for a patient's care are often reached by team discussion and mutual decision.

Although Boston Floating Hospital is an institution entirely for children, parents who stay with them are housed in the Family Participation Unit, which is similar to the Care-by-Parent Unit at the University of Kentucky Medical Center. In both places, the cost per day for the child is lower than in a regular ward: at Boston Floating Hospital the regular cost is reduced by $3.00 per day if the mother is with the child,[1] and at the University of Kentucky Medical Center a 1969 survey showed that the fee for both mother and child, including meals, was approximately 40 percent less than the cost for the child alone in the acute pediatric ward.[2] Since family involvement prevails in all areas of Henrietta Egleston Hospital, no cost comparisons can be made.

A clear picture of the point of view and the atmosphere of such hospitals as these can only be gotten by looking beyond the statistics and charts and seeing and hearing what happens every day.

---

[1]Ross Laboratory. Family-inclusive hospital care for children. *Currents in Hospital Administration* 8:1-4, 1964. Parts 1 and 2.

[2]James, V., and Wheeler, W.   Care-by-Parent Unit. *Pediatrics* 43:488, 1969.

THE HENRIETTA EGLESTON HOSPITAL FOR CHILDREN

Part of the Woodruff Medical Center at Emory University, a large complex embracing clinics, research buildings, and schools, the Henrietta Egleston Hospital for Children cares for children in the metropolitan area as well as taking referrals. Children from newborn age to 16 years old, with all conditions, are admitted for medical observation and treatment. The new 100-bed hospital, opened in 1959, is a pleasant building surrounded by grass and trees, designed for maximum light and informality, and decorated throughout in soft pastel colors. Being a research center as well as a teaching institution, it has close links with Emory University Hospital, Elk's Aidmore Hospital for Convalescent Children, and the Emory University Clinic for mutual use of special facilities.

Since 1928, when Henrietta Egleston Hospital first opened its doors as a 52-bed hospital founded and endowed by a private citizen of Atlanta, it has been characterized by commitment to a very personal kind of care. The board of directors, the administration, and even the maintenance staff tend to be stable, with individuals sometimes remaining with the hospital for thirty or forty years. Volunteer organizations and the community around it have the same kind of long-term interest in its welfare and pride in its achievements.

With the opening of the new building, the policy of living in for parents was inaugurated under the direction of Dr. Joseph H. Patterson, chief physician and professor of pediatrics at the Emory University School of Medicine, and Miss Margaret Bodeker, R.N., director of the Division of Nursing, now retired. Almost no other hospital in the country had such a policy, and from that time until the present writing, Henrietta Egleston Hospital has continually had a great many visitors from other institutions who want to see at firsthand how its policies work and why they are so successful.

From the informal entrance lobby with its glass doors leading to trees and gardens, a family begins to see this hospital as a series of color-paneled hallways, open doors, and large windows with gaily striped curtains. Parents stay with their children in private or semiprivate rooms with their own hand-washing and toilet facilities; there are also four-bed units for patients which parents may visit at any time. Private rooms each have a complete bathroom and a convertible sofa-bed for the parent, along with a rocking chair, a table, and the child's bed or crib. These rooms are allocated on a basis of need rather than on ability to pay.

"Modern as the hospital is, on occasion the space for parents is limited," says Dr. Patterson. "You sell an idea, and if it is a good one, the community comes to expect this as the natural and accepted method of child care." There is no sense of overcrowding, however, although there is ample evidence of parent participation. Children's toys are on shelves and their paintings and crayon drawings decorate the walls and windows. In a private room a child is in bed playing with a puzzle; his father, in a rocking chair beside him, reads the paper as he would at home. Two young mothers who share a room have dressed their baby girls in pretty home clothes and put a blanket on the floor so the babies, propped up on pillows, can look at each other "for company." The mothers are chatting, and a nurse stops by to exchange a few sociable words with them and admire the babies' dresses.

Two nurses outside the large window of a private room stand back so they won't be seen. "Watch out for that tape recorder when you go in," says one with a laugh. "He's bound to get us all to talk into it—his father brought it yesterday."

There is a child activities program and playroom areas on the various floors. Two full-time teachers schedule regular classes. One gets the feeling, however, that these activities are subordinate to the interactions between the parents and children in the rooms. As with the two mothers whose babies were sharing a blanket, the playroom is often wherever the parents happen to be. Mobility is encouraged, and even toddlers and babies, in strollers or walking, go on expeditions down the halls with a parent or a volunteer worker.

The staff uses the daily presence of parents and the many informal contacts as ongoing opportunities for teaching parents how to care for their children and for answering questions about the child's illness.

"The only places where parents do not generally go," said Miss Bodeker, "are the treatment and recovery rooms. Even our premature babies are not housed in a special unit; the mothers come in to learn to care for them."

A staff of social workers working closely with members of the medical and nursing staff help families in understanding the present illness and the emotional stresses and readjustments that accompany illness. They also conduct and participate in patient-care conferences and programs for staff development and serve as liaison between the hospital and numerous local and statewide family and health-related community agencies. A special fund assists with overnight lodging or cot charges for those parents with limited financial resources who come from a long distance.

Parents gather informally in the evenings for bridge games or talk. On occasion there are discussion groups, led by professionals, for parents of children with a common problem. The hospital chaplain also takes active leadership in the support and counseling of parents. His office serves as a place of retreat as well as a meeting place for parent groups.

For the most part, families are helpful and supportive to each other, and a mother who might feel isolated and lonely is often cheered by the presence of others who can understand her worries. Occasionally, differing temperaments or a lack of understanding of medical information can lead to tensions between the adults, but these occasions are infrequent and staff members seem to agree that they are not a major problem.

Observing this established and well-working program, with its excellent and intensive medical care made more reassuring and hopeful by its maintenance of family warmth and normal childhood activities, it is easy to view this hospital as a place where ". . . they all lived happily ever after." However, the underlying message is not really that there is a happy ending; it is rather that in dealing with human beings there is no ending at all. The staff of Henrietta Egleston Hospital, having moved beyond the initial questions of whether to involve parents, how to house them, and how to train personnel in relationships with families—subjects which many hospitals are still debating—is very much concerned with some forward-looking and more subtle problems. One, which is rarely voiced elsewhere, is the new role of the nurse in relation to the parent as well as the child—what the nurse herself feels and identification of areas of stress. Miss Bodeker explained:

It isn't just a question of having a mother here so many hours of the day. The essential ingredient with both the child and the parent is trust. If a mother can be here, and then can feel free to go home for a while and trust us while she is gone, it's better for her and for her child. This is particularly true with long-term and terminally ill patients. Mothers can become exhausted, and we have to help them get away for a while without feeling guilty. We have to be able to help when a mother breaks down and can't handle her own feelings.

It is a prevalent misconception that when parents are with the children the nursing staff has less to do. Our policy was not inaugurated to save time or trouble for the nursing staff; if anything, it adds to the job. We do this because it's better for the children and rewarding for everyone; but it adds a dimension to nursing care, which means that our staff must be more skilled and more aware than ever before.

Miss Cheryl Scofield, M.N.Ed., the present director of the nursing division, is very aware of some of the problems that arise for nurses when they expand their role to embrace relationships with parents as well as their patients, and she has published an article on the subject.[3]

Since mothers are present for many hours of the day, it is easier for nurses to carry out a teaching program with them than it was when all instruction to parents had to be scheduled during limited visiting hours. Miss Scofield thinks that this inevitably leads on occasion to postponement of some teaching, however, particularly during times when the staff is very busy. Some scheduling of parent conferences and teaching procedures is necessary, on as flexible a basis as possible but as a planned part of hospital care.

Parents often ask the same questions many times. This may pose a problem for the nurse, who tries to answer all questions as honestly and informatively as she can, but who can become frustrated if she is repetitively asked a question to which she does not know the answer or one which she feels the doctor should answer. Some doctors allow the nurse to sit in on the doctor-parent conference, which is very

---

[3]Scofield, C. Parents in the hospital. *Nursing Clinics of North America* 4:59-67, 1969.

helpful; other doctors may tell the nurse what they have said to the parents; and some parents discuss with the nurse what the doctor has told them. The parent who continues to ask the same questions may do so from anxiety, indicating a need for support from the nurse. The question of communication can be solved in many ways, but it does remain one of the major problems for those nurses involved in family participation.

At Henrietta Egleston Hospital, nurses are assigned to a specific patient-care unit. Sometimes, though, it is extremely difficult for nurses to tolerate the emotional and physical stress of being on a patient-care unit with several terminally ill children. Miss Scofield is very much aware of the nurses' need to have some time to recuperate and work through their own feelings after a patient has died before becoming involved again in such a state of stress. When it is felt necessary, nurses may be temporarily assigned to another area to give them a rest from working in such an intense situation.

Parents are permitted to assist with treatment and to give as much care to their terminally ill children as they desire and feel qualified to give. When the child appears to be at the final stage of his illness, the nurse usually assumes almost total physical care, and the mother gives up some of her task to the nurse. The supervising personnel of the hospital feel that their chief role in this situation is to work with the nursing staff to ease tensions and perhaps to teach if appropriate occasions arise. The problems of interrelationship between professionals and parents are of ongoing concern to the staff here and are discussed in the hospital's in-service training.

This hospital is fortunate in having an auxiliary of women who are interested in the hospital and have been active in supporting it since 1928. Organizations such as the Atlanta Debutante Club and the Junior League also support the hospital, with fund-raising and with services, and there are volunteer Pink Ladies and Candy Stripers. This interest and activity on the part of the community mean that attractive and homelike touches—flower arrangements, Christmas parties, and extra people on hand to make personal contact with the mothers and children—are very much a part of the hospital and give it an unusually reassuring and cheerful air.

Although there are many small hospitals across the country with cheerful and bright facilities and with willing volunteers, the remarkable quality about Henrietta Egleston Hospital is that it continues to move into new areas of concern for the well-being of the child and his family. In-service training and orientation for the staff are stressed because, in the words of Miss Bodeker and Dr. Patterson, "In order to effectively operate a pediatric hospital and actually apply this philosophy, every person on the staff must feel that this is important and is best for the patient. This feeling, along with some understanding of the basis for the philosophy, must be shared not just by the doctors and nurses, but by people in all departments, from administration through housekeeping." Teaching rounds, total-care conferences, and education of residents, interns, and nursing staff in the emotional and intellectual needs of children are a constant part of the daily life here. An even more unusual facet of the training is the attention given to the feelings and problems of the staff members themselves.

Not every institution could hope to duplicate the fortunate situation, community interest, and excellent facilities of Henrietta Egleston Hospital. But, even here, where one would expect a comfortable reliance on these features and on the smooth functioning of a good pediatric hospital, new questions are being raised, there is involvement in new problems, and the staff is being trained in new ways of thinking.

"I've worked in other places," says one young nurse on the floor. "But you get interested here—you really care. I just wouldn't want to work in any other kind of hospital, after Egleston."

THE CARE-BY-PARENT UNIT, UNIVERSITY OF KENTUCKY MEDICAL CENTER

The Care-by-Parent Unit, which was developed as an inpatient facility in the Department of Pediatrics at the University of Kentucky Medical Center at Lexington in 1966, is guided by the same philosophy of total care as that at Henrietta Egleston Hospital but faces some very different problems.

The difficulties in bringing children into the hospital for treatment, the clannish and nonverbal background of many of the rural families, and often the family's lack of understanding of what constitutes good diet or good health care all contributed to the need for finding some way in which parents could become involved with the hospital long enough to understand and carry out adequate care for their children following discharge.

Dr. Vernon James, director of the unit, was able to take over a ward in the hospital originally planned as an ambulant section for adult patients and to restructure it as a living-in unit for patients and their families. Since the whole program was experimental, several questions arose from the beginning: The first was the question of authority. It was Dr. James's conviction that the final court of appeal must be the doctor, since in any question of responsibility the doctor is ultimately accountable.

The concern as to whether parents from these inaccessible areas would be able to stay was resolved quickly. Of the first 100 patients eligible for admission, less than 5 percent were unable to have a family member with them. It is the policy of the pediatric department never to insist that a family member stay; the hospital has a conventional pediatric ward. But on the Care-by-Parent Unit someone must stay with the child at all times. The requirement as to who actually stays is flexibly interpreted (one mother brought twins to the hospital with her, although only one child was sick); sometimes a father, an older sibling, or some other family member whom the child trusts will stay.

The question of legal responsibility was also a serious consideration. Since the parents would be responsible for care at all times, even when no hospital staff was on the unit, the possibility of lawsuits against the hospital was very real. In the six years since the unit's inception, however, there have been no court actions. As a preventive measure the public was completely informed about the operation of the unit when it first opened, and parents are clearly apprised of their responsibility upon admission of their child. Dr. James is convinced that fear of possible lawsuits should not be a deterrent to such a program. In fact, his respect for the expertise of the parents and their sense of responsibility is unshakable.

The Care-by-Parent Unit occupies one wing of the hospital, on the same floor with the other pediatric facilities. It is adjacent to the pediatric outpatient clinic, of which it is administratively a part, and uses those facilities and treatment rooms for procedures. The unit consists of 15 private rooms, each with a studio-couch bed for the mother and a bed or crib for the child. Each room has a private bathroom with a shower; the bathrooms have medicine cabinets that are placed out of children's reach and can be locked, so that the mother can keep the child's medications at hand. On the door of each bathroom is a simple map of the unit with the particular room marked in red, to orient the mother to her surroundings.

At the end of the hall, always open, is a kitchen with a stove, refrigerator, washing machine and dryer, iron and ironing board, and bathinette. Parents may use it at any time, and often several make use of it together. Regular meals for the parent and child are delivered to the unit on individual trays; the kitchen is supplementary.

The entrance area of the unit, at the opposite end of the hall, is used as a common room for the parents and children. The nurses' desk is there, and the furniture is comfortable and informal, with toys and games for the children and magazines and ashtrays on the tables for their parents. Often the area is decorated specially for holidays or with some of the children's handiwork.

Because patients come from rural areas, and sometimes from not easily accessible mountain regions, a large map in the common room gives parents the opportunity to identify to the doctors and nurses the localities from which they come and at the same time to orient themselves to the geographic relationship of the hospital to their homes. Each patient's name is put in the appropriate location on the map with a colored pin.

Dr. James says of these parents: "We have very concerned parents here, parents who are intelligent, who want to do the right thing for their children, but who often have no idea what to do. Often they have very low incomes and very little education. They are capable of learning a great deal about how to care for the children and are eager to learn it—but how can you reach them? It's very difficult to take the services out to such a scattered area, so we had the idea of bringing the parents to stay here, where they could keep close family ties and still be learning."

Families are often specifically encouraged to come into the unit, if the staff feels that working with the mother or father is an important factor in the child's care. Adolescents, on the other hand, rarely stay in the unit, since they are not dependent on the parent's presence and since it is sometimes helpful to them to be emotionally as well as physically separated from the family.

Once housed in the Care-by-Parent Unit, mothers take entire care of the children, including the carrying out of routine hospital procedures. They take temperatures, keep charts, do 24-hour urine collections (which, according to Dr. James, are sometimes done more efficiently in the unit than on the acute pediatric ward), give medicines, sometimes take blood pressures, and often in addition learn to carry out more complicated procedures. No nurses are assigned exclusively to the unit; the nursing staff of the outpatient clinic, with the help of Child Care Assistants, is responsible for instructing and supervising the parents. They teach procedures, watch the mothers carry them out under supervision until their competence is assured, and make twice-daily rounds from the clinic nearby to help, to advise, and to give medical care beyond the parents' abilities. Four Child Care Assistants, specially trained aides with experience on pediatric wards, alternate on duty between 6 A.M. and 10:30 P.M. to teach, to see that procedures are followed and hospital appointments are kept, and to befriend and reassure the parents. They are trained by the clinic nurses and the medical director of the unit.

Before admission to the Care-by-Parent Unit, families are given a booklet which addresses itself to the child, although there is a short page of factual information for parents. The booklet is illustrated with simple drawings for the child to color, and the cover reads "Bring this book to the hospital— we have crayons to color it." The information inside is written simply and directly, with a space to write in the date of the child's admission, pictures of some of the people he will see, and a few basic questions that the doctor will ask him. The print is larger than that of most admission booklets and is more widely spaced. This format is used not only to acquaint the child in a simple, straightforward way with what he can expect, but to inform parents who may have only elementary reading skills. This is one example of the care that has gone into making the unit informal for both parents and children; another example are the blue and white checked uniforms of the Child Care Assistants, who are thus easily recognizable as distinct from the nursing staff.

Soon after a mother's arrival, a Child Care Assistant acquaints her with the unit, explains the daily routine, and introduces her to other families. As they become familiar with their surroundings, mothers will chat in the common room or gather in the kitchen-laundry room to talk while they do housework. Dr. James says, "The really important feature of this unit is the coffeepot—it's used all day long, and we couldn't run the place without it." There are occasional parties that all parents and some of the staff attend, and some mothers have used the kitchen to cook special dinners with supplies brought in from outside the hospital.

Although this casual atmosphere might give the newcomer an impression that the unit is a convalescent ward or handles only very minor illnesses, the opposite is true. The patients here have included a high percentage with cardiac and neurological problems. The caseload ranges from premature infants to children who are mentally retarded, have birtn defects, or are undergoing plastic surgery. Mothers are taught to do procedures involving a high degree of skill and responsibility; one mother who had had no formal education was taught how to give her child insulin and mastered the technique in just five days. Some have cared for tracheostomy tubes, and some have been taught to monitor blood transfusions and keep meticulous records. All pediatric specialties and many surgical subspecialties have been represented in this unit.

Dr. James is convinced that one of the great advantages of the Care-by-Parent Unit is that there is opportunity not only to teach the parent needed skills and to supervise the practice of them, but at the same time to observe the family interaction so that both parent and child can be strengthened and supported.

Premature babies, for instance, are admitted to the unit with their mothers two or three days before they are ready to go home, so that the mother, under supervision, can take over the complete care of the baby. Sometimes the public health nurse from the mother's home county will visit and participate in the instructions given by the clinic nurse to the mothers, thus insuring continuance of support for the mother and child at home. In every case, the physician, clinic nurse, and Child Care Assistant can take time while the mother is in the unit to give her the skills and confidence she needs to take the baby home without fear.

Social workers and students in social work help the children to express their feelings and help the parents to a better understanding of themselves and their families. The staff psychiatrist occasionally admits a mother and child to the unit in order to observe how they relate to each other and to help them deal with emotional as well as physical problems. The staff has found that the use of the Care-by-Parent Unit as a diagnostic facility is not only an extremely efficient way to gain a total observation of the child as a part of the family, but that it often saves involved and expensive laboratory diagnostic tests. Says Dr. James:

We are concerned about failure-to-thrive children. We have found that we can bring them in here and find within a day or two that the mother is not even feeding the child—no wonder he fails to thrive! The first day, a mother may show us how well she cares for her baby. By the second day, she begins to feel at home here and starts treating him more the way she does at home. By the third day, she may have lost interest in him and be entirely neglecting him. We can see it happen. It's a beautiful diagnostic setup that doesn't cost anything in laboratory fees and saves all kinds of time and money. The same thing is sometimes true of the battered child. When we have a child in the general pediatrics section whom we have reason to believe is a battered child, we try to get the mother or father here—both, if possible—for the last few days of the child's stay. Here again, we can observe the careful behavior the first day and then the parents' reverting to the way they ordinarily treat him. Our psychiatrist and our psychiatric resident can spot this very soon. It's a very good, very simple diagnostic procedure.

Sometimes parents can be helpful in reassuring other parents, and particularly in keeping other mothers from feeling isolated and alone. Parents will baby-sit for each other and arrange to trade time-off. They meet, talk, and have coffee together to bridge the times of anxious waiting. Like the nursing staff at Henrietta Egleston Hospital, the Child Care Assistants here are alert for the possibility of parents giving each other misinformation or of frightening each other, but this happens rarely.

A question that sometimes arises is whether the Care-by-Parent Unit complicates the work of the staff and whether it is an additional burden for the medical personnel. The residents, interns, and medical students rotate through this unit and through general pediatrics as part of their regular program. They frequently express the feeling that there is more time to take an interest in family problems in the Care-by-Parent Unit than in the conventional unit, which leads to discussion with the staff and often to changes in attitude toward all patients and their families.

Dr. James reported that this unit was the first choice for medical students in their junior year. One resident currently on the unit was more specific: "You see things here—long-term illnesses and families dealing with such problems—that you often wouldn't have any experience with until you went into private practice. You are able to see facets of illnesses that just aren't apparent when you are dealing with a patient on a general acute unit. It's interesting to get to know the families; you find you're really concerned with the people." There are also indications that the surgical staff has a new awareness of the importance of talking to the parents and children about imminent surgery. Some who had doubts about the ability of the mothers to care for their children now welcome the opportunity to have them housed in this unit.

On the general pediatrics wards at the University of Kentucky Medical Center, the average stay of a patient is 9 to 11 days, while on the Care-by-Parent Unit the average stay is 4.2 days. The length of hospitalization also compares favorably with the number of visits to the outpatient clinic that would be necessary for evaluation and diagnostic procedures. It is far easier for parents who would have difficulties with transportation to stay with the child than to bring him for successive visits; it is efficient for staff as well.

The nurses, who divide their time between the outpatient clinic and the unit, and the Child Care Assistants sometimes find that simultaneous demands on their time and attention can be a problem. Recently, a ward clerk has been hired to handle telephone calls, routine scheduling, and messages, freeing the Child Care Assistants to spend more time with parents and children. The absence of full-time professional nurses, except for twice-daily rounds, has increased the concern of the nursing staff for teaching and supervising the mothers. Further impetus for this kind of teaching has been given by the evidence that the mothers are very capable of carrying out instructions once they are made clear. The staff members, at the same time, have become increasingly aware of their own capabilities in communicating with parents, since there is time and opportunity to observe whether the parent has understood clearly or whether further teaching is necessary.

The unit is thus a sort of two-way laboratory in which residents, interns, nurses, and Child Care Assistants learn to perfect their own skills in dealing with the family and with the total well-being of the child and in which the ability to watch the child and parent interacting together offers great opportunity for observation and research. An added dimension is the awareness both of growth stages in their children and of health practices that families take back to their own communities. As this program matures and expands, it is obvious that new ways of using the unit for the support of families and the education of professionals are emerging. But for the parents who bring their children to the hospital, the pervading feature is the warmth and personal interest.

"Sometimes, if I'm off duty, I'll come in for a little while just to take a mother out to see the streets," says a Child

Care Assistant. "Some of them come from way out in the country, and the city is really scary for them."

"Hold your horses, Mary. I'm coming in after I look at the chart a minute," a white-coated resident tells a little girl. "I said you can go home today, but I have to take a look at you first." The child is swinging herself by both hands in the doorway and giggling.

"Bye-bye, baby." A father and two little boys are leaving, but mother and little brother are staying. When the baby's face puckers and he is about to cry, the mother slings him onto one hip, as she does at home, and takes him over to the drinking fountain to see the pretty water. He is diverted and begins to laugh.

No barred cribs and lonely children are in sight. A young father is rolling his own cigarette from paper and the contents of a tobacco sack while he talks to his wife, who is holding their 2-year-old. They are serious and worried, but they are a family, together, not a case history in an institution.

BOSTON FLOATING HOSPITAL FOR INFANTS AND CHILDREN

Unlike Henrietta Egleston Hospital and the University of Kentucky Medical Center, Boston Floating Hospital is surrounded by city streets and has a larger caseload, with a clientele from the urban population as well as patients from other states and countries who have been referred because of the hospital's many specialties. It cares for children from infancy to 21 years of age and has teaching connections with Tufts University's Schools of Medicine and Dental Medicine.

The Tufts University-New England Medical Center complex, of which Boston Floating Hospital is a part, is currently building a new $72 million development which will provide some much-needed space. At present, the hospital has 100 beds and many health services—outpatient clinics are crowded with parents and children throughout the daytime hours—in a facility built in 1931 and which has since been only partially remodeled.

The first impetus for a unit in which parents could live in with their children came from the play program established in 1947. Unlike most play programs, this one is administratively a part of the inpatient Psychiatric Service for Children. Its emphasis from its inception was on making the child's illness a less traumatic experience for both the parent and the child. This program has had an important role in the training of pediatricians as well as those interested in children's mental health, and its playroom has been used increasingly for the treatment of children with certain specific emotional disturbances. The role of the play program and of general pediatrics at Boston Floating Hospital is discussed in other sections of this book. The Family Participation Unit, which was opened in 1963, concerns us here since it, like the University of Kentucky Medical Center's Care-by-Parent Unit, specifically involves parents who stay in the unit and actively participate in nursing care.

Boston Floating Hospital's unit, under the direction of Dr. William Rothney, director of Inpatient Psychiatric Services for Children of the New England Medical Center Hospitals, was converted from a nurses' residential section of the hospital and is a self-contained department which makes use of the wider facilities of the hospital while it carries out a specific policy of its own. It opened with 4 rooms for parent and child. Since that time it has been expanded to a 9-room unit with a staff of six registered nurses and a nurse leader. Each of the rooms, like those in the Care-by-Parent Unit, has a bed for the mother and the child, a dressing table-desk, and a comfortable chair. There are also tubs and a shower room which serve the unit.

A central hall with a nurses' desk serves as an informal center for mothers and has tables and chairs for meals. The kitchen, which opens from this hall, has complete facilities, and parents are encouraged to bring some of their children's favorite foods and prepare them, although the hospital provides regularly scheduled meals. Parents themselves have their meals in the cafeteria and sometimes bring in food from outside. The hospital supplies tea, coffee, and toast for parents in the kitchen as a routine service of the unit. A small separate common room, which serves as living room and playroom, has comfortable chairs, toys, books, and a television set.

Although the unit is not spacious, the atmosphere is casual and friendly. Set apart from the normal routine of the hospital, the tempo seems relaxed and unobstructed, with mothers coming in and out of the rooms, chatting as casually with the nurses on duty as they do with each other, and using the facility in an almost proprietary, homelike way. Very similar in many ways to the Care-by-Parent Unit, this unit differs in that a nursing staff is assigned regularly to the service and there is no supplementary system of aides. The mothers support each other a good deal, even baby-sitting for each other on occasion. The staff encourages parents to leave for short intervals, even going out for dinner when the children are asleep, in order to lead as normal a life as possible. Two nurses are on duty, except in the evening; after hours a registered nurse or a licensed practical nurse is always on the unit, and there is an emergency telephone on which to call the resident if necessary.

An afternoon in the Family Participation Unit is very like

a casual neighborhood visit except for the pervading atmosphere of concern for the children, most of whom are toddlers; many have surgical dressings in evidence or are confined to low, wheeled reclining carts called couch-carts in which they can be moved about. In the living room, a father is visiting his wife and child. While they talk, the child is watching television with the sound turned low. The father can smoke, the mother is in a print house-dress; they are keeping an eye on the child, but there seems to be no tension over his condition.

A child wanders in and out of the living room; his mother is at the table in the center hall talking with a third mother over a cup of coffee. Nearby another young mother, in slacks and a blouse, holds her little boy on her lap while he tries to make her taste his grape Popsicle by holding it to her mouth. She is restraining him gently, careful of his bandaged head, while she occasionally joins the conversation at the table. In the kitchen there are cups on the drainboard and the instant coffee jar is in evidence. At the desk where the records are kept, a young nurse is telephoning. She is not in uniform since all the nurses on this unit wear street clothes, and from the mothers' conversation it is evident that her position in their eyes is a little different from that in the ordinary nurse-parent relationship.

"I don't think she's had a minute to sit down," says one mother. "Her relief was late or something, and she's been on the go all day."

The nurse has finished her call and tells the other mother, "You can take him down now. They're ready for you." As the mother gets up to wheel her child in his couch-cart out of the unit, there is some direction and explanation.

"You're sure you know where to go?"

"I went there yesterday. And it's about time they're ready!"

The nurse and the mother laugh together with the same note of indulgence. Mothers on this unit may accompany their children to all areas of the hospital—therapy rooms, x-ray, and so on—although a nurse accompanies the mother and child if the child has had preoperative medication. The nurse is also available to help mothers who seem overly anxious or hesitant about the responsibility.

At the table, a mother says, "Thursday night we had a ball. I'll bet we were up all night. We decided to send out for Chinese food, then sat around and talked half the night; it turned into a real party."

Criticism seems to be at about the same level as in a neighborhood or nursery school, despite the realistic anxiety that the parents feel about the children. "Once in a while it gets bad in here. One night we were all up, and everybody was upset . . ."

"That was the night the little boy had a convulsion," another adds. "It was all right after a while, but it just seemed to get to everybody."

"You shouldn't try to do all that," a mother tells the nurse. "Why don't you leave some of it? You ought to have been off by now anyway." She uses an older-sister tone of indulgence, very different from the tone one would usually take with a figure of authority.

"I think part of it is because we don't wear a uniform," the nurse explains later. "Sometimes it's more work on the whole in here, but it's very rewarding work. The whole unit makes me feel much more like a friend to the parents than I would working on a regular unit."

The parents carry out home-style care of the children and are responsible for keeping charts and giving routine medications. They are first instructed by the nurses in the procedures to follow and are supervised until they feel competent to carry them out alone. They then take full responsibility—asking for help only if they feel it necessary—except for the more difficult and technical procedures done only by the nurses. Many diabetic children learn to care for themselves in this unit, with the mothers coached in ways of helping them and of encouraging them to take responsibility for themselves.

Fathers as well as mothers have lived in with the children and have very successfully "mothered" and supported them. On occasion an older sibling has come with the child, and that too has been successful. Parents are given a choice between this unit and hospitalization on a regular ward for the child, since the parent's ability to help with care and withstand stress are important factors in successful living in. In some cases, the physician will try, for therapeutic or diagnostic reasons, to influence the choice in order to have the mother with the child. Children in acute stages of illness or who need special equipment often cannot be admitted.

There has been a gradual change of emphasis in the philosophy of the Family Participation Unit since its inception, according to Dr. Rothney. It was never inaugurated as a money-saving program and was first conceived as primarily a unit where mothers could be with their children and help with nursing care. The major criterion for admission now is whether the presence of the parent is thought to be of particular value to the child in coping with hospitalization and the kind and variety of treatment he would be undergoing. Specific needs of the family, the ability to cope with stress, and the child's needs and best interests are all considered.

A social group worker meets with parents individually and in groups, with children, and with staff to help with living-in problems on the unit and with home and personal problems. Because the mothers as well as the children need reassurance and support, the medical staff, nurses, and social group worker function as an interdisciplinary team. The particular importance of the social group worker is that she can often deal with the parents' feelings by holding informal meetings of all the parents and by making frequent casual contacts; she can also pass along to the medical and nursing staff some information learned from the parents. In addition, she is of great value to all the parents as a group in helping them in times of crisis. In the few instances of death in the Family Participation Unit, the social group worker, Miss Beverly Sun, has been able to help with the feelings and fears of all the parents and to resolve some of the tensions and sorrow into a mutually supportive atmosphere. With her help the parents as a group are often able to come to decisions about what to tell their children or how to best help each other.

The quality of interaction with parents on the Family Participation Unit has interested the nursing staff in other sections of the hospital. At their request, Dr. Rothney is now meeting weekly for an hour with the nurses of each ward to help them put into effect some of the kinds of parent support used in this unit. He also holds meetings with the unit staff three times a week, since it has a particularly demanding role: carrying out nursing care and helping mothers with their emotions and with the physical care of their children.

Dr. Rothney would like to see more such units in the hospital, with screening done for similarities of family background, similar illnesses of the patients, and common interests of parents; this would thus make for less diversity among the parents and thus easier understanding and more mutual support, thereby lessening the burden of the nursing staff. He is also convinced that one very real problem in centers, such as Boston Floating Hospital, which give many kinds of specialized care is the danger of losing track of the child's identity by centering interest on his illness. At present, the Family Participation Unit is under divided jurisdiction; even a child who is doing well there may be removed at the discretion of a specialist who may lack sympathy with or understanding of the child's emotional and growth needs. One solution to this problem, says Dr. Rothney, would be to reinstate the family physician, who would have an ongoing relationship with the child and family and would take into consideration the family situation and the child's emotional state. The specialists could then decide, in cooperation with the family doctor, the best plan for the care of a particular child.

No program of this kind can thrive or even gain a foothold without the underlying support of the hospital administration. In the case of the Family Participation Unit, Miss Geneva Katz, R.N., Administrator of Boston Floating Hospital, has provided the cooperation and assistance that established and continues to maintain the project.

SUMMARY

Problems such as these concern the staff of the Family Participation Unit, with emphasis on the emotional factors, in both children and parents, of illness and the effects of having many specialties in the hospital. At the Care-by-Parent Unit at the University of Kentucky Medical Center, the emphasis is centered around concern for its rural patients and the tenuous communication with low-income families in inaccessible areas. The Henrietta Egleston Hospital is oriented toward educating nurses in new ways of handling their expanded role with parents and children. Despite these differences in emphasis, the same basic approach to the child as an individual and as a member of a family is the underlying theme of all three facilities. And despite the problems which they face in pioneering new kinds of care, the atmosphere of each is infinitely more human than that of most traditional hospitals.

REFERENCES

Aufhauser, T. Parent participation in hospital care of children. *Nursing Outlook* 15:40-42, 1967.

Bright, F. The pediatric nurse and parental anxiety. *Nursing Forum* 4:30-47, 1965.

Fagin, C. The case for rooming-in when young children are hospitalized. *Nursing Science* 2:324-333, 1964.

Fagin, C. *Effect of Maternal Attendance During Hospitalization on Post-Hospital Behavior.* Philadelphia: F. A. Davis, 1966.

Katz, G. Mothers can help sick children in experimental unit. *Hospitals,* July 1, 1964.

Mahaffy, P., Jr. Nurse-parent relationships in living-in situations. *Nursing Forum* 3:53-64, 1964.

Seidl, F., and Pilliterri, A. Development of an attitude scale on parent participation. *Nursing Research* 16:71-73, 1967.

Shore, M. F. (Ed.). *Red Is the Color of Hurting.* Bethesda, Md.: National Institute of Mental Health, 1967.

Wessel, M., and La Camera, R. Care by parent, further advantages. *Pediatrics* 44:303, 1969.

3

Planning for Parents

THE three hospitals just discussed make available complete rooms for housing a parent and a child together and are structured to give the parent an active, full-time role in the child's care. These units are all separated from the traditional wards and no child is admitted to them without a parent or parent surrogate.

However, more usual, and with a different set of aims and problems, is the unit which includes mothers (and sometimes other members of the child's family) on the ordinary pediatric ward. In some hospitals arrangements for the presence of mothers and fathers are preplanned and the facilities are particularly well suited to include them. In others, parent facilities are fitted into whatever spaces can be utilized and are, of course, less convenient for the staff as well as for the parent.

Two large hospitals which illustrate particularly well what can be achieved by planning facilities for parent involvement in a general pediatrics unit are The Johns Hopkins Hospital in Baltimore and the University of Colorado Medical Center in Denver. The pediatricians-in-chief at both hospitals have implemented active programs for living in even though separate rooms for mother and child are not available except under unusual circumstances.

These two hospitals are similar in many other ways. Both have fairly new pediatric facilities: the Children's Medical and Surgical Center at The Johns Hopkins Hospital was opened in 1963 and the Colorado General Hospital of the University of Colorado Medical Center in 1965. Both are large, complex hospitals with many disciplines and serve not only the major cities in which they are located, but also handle patients from other states and even other countries. More importantly, each has a pediatrician-in-chief convinced of the need for a concept of total care. Dr. Robert E. Cooke at The Johns Hopkins Hospital and Dr. Henry Kempe, chairman of the Department of Pediatrics, and Dr. Henry Silver, professor of pediatrics, at the University of Colorado General Hospital have inaugurated and implemented new ways of caring for children and have set the tone for their departments, which now take for granted the importance of child development and of meeting emotional and cognitive needs.

CHILDREN'S MEDICAL AND SURGICAL CENTER, THE JOHNS HOPKINS HOSPITAL

Within the bewilderingly large complex of The Johns Hopkins Hospital, which dominates the slum area of Baltimore that surrounds it and is like a city within a city, the Children's Medical and Surgical Center is a self-contained and multiple totality, yet another city contained in the larger whole. The long halls of the main floor, with bewildering signs and lounges, are filled with a steadily moving crowd of medical professionals and patients; from here, a handsome entry area gives access to the elevators to the 8 floors of the Children's Center, all devoted to every phase of the care of children. Four floors have playrooms which are also used as school and dining areas, and the sixth floor short-term unit has a small play area.

The Center included in its building plans facilities for eighty parents to stay overnight at any one time. There is no charge. Three floors have shower and dressing-room units with ample space, good lighting, and a dressing table; these facilities are also used by those who stay on the floors between. Lounge chairs with ottomans that, pushed together, convert into cots are available on 5 floors. On the babies and toddlers' floor, which includes the premature babies unit, there is one sleeping unit with three cubicles for mothers, each opposite a baby's crib; each has curtains for privacy, a bed, and a bedside table. Mothers often do their children's preoperative scrub in unit bathtubs that have been raised to a convenient height. In addition to children's playrooms, open areas on every floor are set aside for parents. These are attractively furnished with comfortable chairs, sofas, and a coffee table and decorated with plants.

The parent who brings a child to The Johns Hopkins Hospital is first introduced to the policy of the hospital through the preadmission booklet prepared by the Child Life Department, a special department administratively within the Department of Pediatrics. The introduction, written by Dr. Cooke, is unusual in its sympathetic understanding of parents' feelings.

Parents are probably the most abused people on earth. If their children are ill, they may be considered neglectful. If they are well, the parents receive no credit. If a child does poorly in school, the parents are to blame for pushing too much or too little. If he does well, it is because the child is brilliant and has worked hard. No credit is given to the suffering mother and father. But I think parents are great, and I believe that most of them are willing to make tremendous efforts and sacrifices to help their children.

. . . We must count on the help of parents even at a time when they are most anxious and most concerned . . .

. . . The success or failure of a child's adjustment to the hospital is directly related to the reactions of his family to this experience . . . That is why we want you to be here with your child helping us as much as possible. We feel that if the parent knows what this hospital is all about, he or she will explain to the child much of what goes on far better than any of us can . . .

. . . We want you as a member of the hospital team; it will help your child's recovery . . .

The booklet then explains hospital procedure from admission through to hospital routine. After the various floors are described, there is a page of information for the parent who wishes to stay for the night, listing the facilities, describing the role of the Living-In Coordinator, and suggesting clothes that would be most comfortable. Visiting hours are listed for the various floors, but these are more flexible than the pamphlet would suggest since special arrangements are made in many individual cases. Visiting the Children's Center at almost any hour, one is impressed by the number of parents in evidence, either in the waiting areas or engaged in caring for the children. The booklet lists, finally, a glossary of the medical initials and terms that a parent might want clarified, a bibliography of children's books helpful in explaining hospitalizations, and key telephone numbers the parent might need.

It is a remarkable booklet in that it emphasizes hospital facilities from the point of view of the parents making use of them. Other hospital pamphlets are often titled with only the name of the hospital or with the word *Admissions* and then the hospital name. One or two seem to indicate an usurpation of the parent's role—*Your Child—Our Patient, Your Child in the Hospital.* In contrast, this booklet is titled *You and Your Child at the Children's Center,* an implication that the child and parent are both experiencing the hospitalization and are making use of the facility together. The text phrasing is much the same; some of it is subtle, but unmistakable.

Mealtime is an important part of the total child-care program and special pediatric dieticians plan attractive, well-balanced meals that appeal to young patients . . .

. . . As always, you are welcome, too. At mealtime, you can help your child by showing your approval of the food served to him. Even though it may not appeal to you as a grown-up, it is an important part of your child's medical care, particularly if his doctor has ordered a special diet.

Your child's appetite may decrease when he is sick, and the strangeness of the hospital may take away all his interest in food. But unless there is a special medical reason for eating all the food served, it is generally necessary only to encourage your child to taste everything and to eat as much as he can; he will know the amount that is right for him. Because desserts are considered an important part of a balanced diet, they are not withheld even if the rest of the meal is not finished . . .

It seems obvious that this booklet was written with a purpose beyond that of merely making parents familiar with the hospital services and routines. It can serve as a textbook to augment the learning experience of the mother while the child is hospitalized, giving her clues to becoming part of the team, to what behaviors and attitudes are appropriate in various situations, as well as some guides to the child's behavior.

The parent who wishes to live in with the child is under the care of the Living-In Coordinator, a post within the nursing department. The requirements for this position stress a background in child and family development and preparation in psychology and sociology. One of the major responsibilities of the job is "to further the emotional, intellectual, and social development of mothers while they reside in the Center. Work includes orienting and interpreting to medical, nursing, and auxiliary staffs reasons for mothers living in with young children who are hospitalized."

Mrs. Polly Hesterberg, the Living-In Coordinator, is a nurse and finds this training helpful in reassuring mothers and helping them understand the medical care. She meets with each mother soon after the child's admission and, in addition to explaining routines and answering questions, she supplies a map of the first floor of the hospital showing areas outside the Children's Center that may be useful to parents. On the map the hours of the cafeteria are listed as well as its location, and there are clear directions for finding the library, sun deck, information desk, telephones, canteen, outside shops, and even the tennis courts. In addition to this first interview, Mrs. Hesterberg makes rounds every day to talk with the parents and answer questions; she also conducts weekly parent discussion groups.

Parents who stay over fairly long periods often find the waiting times hard to tolerate, says Mrs. Hesterberg. For that reason, an arrangement has been made with the Public Relations Department by which the parents may do volunteer work in the office or library as a relief from inaction on the ward. Many parents are grateful for this opportunity and for the contact it gives them with other adults, away from the stress of the medical setting.

In addition to the Living-In Coordinator, the Child Life

Department, and the policy of concern for parents which is part of the education of the nursing staff, parents have an additional resource in Patients' Staff Services, paid hostesses who serve the entire hospital. On duty every day but Sunday, these hostesses are available to help with outside housing information, with shopping, and with translation services for non-English-speaking families.

Any hospital of this size and complexity can be awe-inspiring and frightening to a parent and child; the crowded elevators and halls, the many pediatric floors, and the variety of medical professionals of all kinds wearing different uniforms and insignia, all combine to make first impressions very bewildering. What is noteworthy about the Children's Center in its approach to families is the realistic view that it takes of this problem. The admissions booklet, the areas on each floor to accommodate parents of children in that particular unit, the special Living-In Coordinator who makes personal contact with the parents, all tend to divide the great anonymity of the hospital into more specific, smaller, and less awesome units. Parents here become acquainted with other small groups of parents and can find their way through the halls with the aid of clearly marked maps or with the help of pleasant hostesses manning many small information desks. Although the Children's Medical and Surgical Center, with its large caseloads and its multiplicity of services, can never wholly give an impression of informality and intimacy, it is remarkable that it has, with much care and insight, put so much emphasis on the small things that loom largest to families of hospitalized children.

The mother is usually the parent who stays with the child, but there are instances of a father or other family member being included in the Living-In Program, demonstrating the flexibility of the program even though the Children's Center has a very large caseload. The living-in mother census alone for August 1968 to September 1969 totalled 1,062.

Mrs. Hesterberg's role as liaison with and educator of staff, nursing students, and volunteers has equal and sometimes greater importance than her work with parents. She serves on medical, nursing, and auxiliary staff committees, plans in-service education programs on living in, and takes out into the community, whenever possible, information on the availability of the living-in facilities. And finally, when a patient who needs special equipment after hospitalization is sent home, Mrs. Hesterberg shares with the nursing staff the responsibility of making sure that the mother or another family member is taught how to handle the equipment and care for the child. The social service department cooperates in the follow-up at home. The assistant director of the social work department says, "As long as our hospital is involved with medical care, we stay involved—whether the patient is an inpatient or outpatient."

To understand the Children's Center policy of involving parents, one must go back to the 1930's. At that time, medical and psychiatric journals began publishing studies on the effects of hospitalization on children. In common with many other hospitals, The Johns Hopkins Hospital then began to develop new attitudes about, and ways of dealing with, their child patients. In 1944 a demonstration play program was started under the auspices of the Child Development Department of Hood College; it soon expanded and became a permanent program, Play Activities. The program engaged a staff of preschool teachers and later moved on to include a school program for older children. As recognition grew of the importance of the parents' role, Dr. Cooke expanded the program still further, renaming it the Child Life Department to better reflect the scope of its activities. These are now based on a twofold philosophy: the concept of family-centered pediatric care and the education of medical and nursing students, technicians, and other professionals in working with the hospitalized child.

The Child Life Department today, administratively within the Department of Pediatrics, is concerned with, and part of, all the pediatric medical, surgical, and nursing services in the outpatient areas as well as in the inpatient department. Although the primary concern of the Child Life Department staff is with the play and school programs and with creating a setting in which children have an optimum opportunity for growth within the hospital setting, their work is closely linked with that of the medical and nursing staff.

Two factors seem to have influenced the impressive growth of this program. First is the interest and commitment on the part of the administration and staff, who, from the highest positions down, translated their interest and concern into implementing working programs. This has made inter-departmental communication an accepted reality. The problems of rotating staff and changing shifts of nurses and assistants, the time factors of a large caseload, and those problems attendant on the fact that The Johns Hopkins Hospital is also a teaching hospital do all contribute to a lack of complete communication and in some areas to a certain amount of frustration, but the policy is nevertheless carried out to a very great degree.

Second, the Child Life Department holds meetings with the heads of other departments, with pediatric house staff and pediatric surgeons, and has regular meetings with fourth-year medical students during their five-week duty in pediatrics. During these meetings they discuss the department's role in the hospital and the effects of hospitalization on children and their families.

A scheduled morning report is given each day to the department staff by the head nurses of the units, to facilitate the day's planning for each floor in general and for individual patients. At this time the nurses and department staff are able to share and discuss their observations of a child and his parents and to formulate plans cooperatively.

The Child Life Department staff also attends floor team conferences and takes part in all multidisciplinary conferences; it is represented on the Children's Medical and Surgical Center Care Committee. It participates in pediatric educational group staff meetings and has frequent contacts and exchanges of information with social service, child psychiatry, and occupational therapy staff.

This interweaving of concern for the child as a person as well as a case history would not be possible without the encouragement of administration and top-level medical staff. As a result, such programs as living in for parents have not only received tacit support; they have become physical fact in the pediatric facility, with beds, showers, lounges, telephones, and so on.

Another factor that has played a major role in the development of a family-centered policy is the work of the Women's Board of the Hospital, which provided financial support for the Play Activities Program at its inception and has continued to be a major financial support of the department as well as supplying some of the volunteers who work in the program. Although supplementary funding augments the budget of the department, the Women's Board continues to be its mainstay. It is an extremely active organization and carries out many volunteer jobs in the hospital as well as staffing a gift shop and snack restaurant, the proceeds from which are used for varied projects. For more than nine years the Child Life Department has been one of these projects.

THE UNIVERSITY OF COLORADO MEDICAL CENTER

The University of Colorado Medical Center, opened to inpatients in 1965, is an extremely handsome, modern complex with many services—including research and medical—and nursing and dental schools, surrounded by trees and landscaped areas. The population of the hospital, which has a maximum capacity of 479 beds, is drawn not only from the surrounding city of Denver, but from an extremely wide area that often includes parts of adjacent states. The pediatric division was planned for the accommodation of parents as well as young patients and has many features not duplicated in any other institution studied. One of the features most notable about the entire area is the general feeling of informality and cheer: nurses on some pediatric units do not wear uniforms, units are well lit, and toys and children's drawings are much in evidence.

The introduction of a family to the pediatric division begins with a booklet directed specifically toward parents. In a simple blue cover, it contains information about the hospital and some directive suggestions. Inside the cover, for instance, a list "Your Child's Doctors Are:" has space for three names: the intern, the resident, and the attending physician. The patient thus has a permanent record of the names for identification. Inside the booklet itself are clear maps of the hospital and the pediatric floor, with entrances marked. In addition, there are specific directions on how to go from place to place as well as a listing of the corridor markings in the pediatric division and where each corridor leads. On the cover a map shows the location of, and approaches to, the hospital. The usual information about room assignments and what clothing and possessions to bring with the child includes this paragraph:

There are several beds available for parents who wish to stay overnight with their children. In the 3-10 year and Infant Unit these beds are located in the child's room. It is very reassuring to the child to have a parent close by during the night. Check with the nurse to see if you may stay with your child. There is no charge for the use of these beds and you are encouraged to use them if they are available.

Under the heading *Health Team,* there is a fairly detailed description of every staff member who will be in contact with the child and his family. The listed health team includes the public health nurse, the social worker, the children's activities coordinator, the teacher, and the dietician, as well as doctors. The role of the social worker is stressed as a service of which the parents may avail themselves.

Social Worker: The medical social workers on the Children's Units are available to children admitted to the hospital and to their parents. Some of the services available include:

1. Enabling the family and the child to deal with problems which may arise during hospitalization or following discharge.

2. Help in locating resources which may assist the patient or his family.

3. Contribute to the doctors' understanding of those social factors which may influence the child's health, care and recovery.

In describing the Intensive Therapy Unit, the booklet lists visiting hours—15 minutes out of every hour—and tells parents that the child may bring one favorite toy with him, marked with his name. It adds, "Specialized equipment is available to aid in your child's care. Please feel free to ask the nurse about any equipment being used with your child." This is the only example found in any patient information booklet of encouraging parents to ask for information about unfamiliar equipment, as well as the only pediatric intensive care unit to which a child is specifically encouraged to bring a toy. There are also instructions on the washing-up procedure on entering or leaving the unit, as a supplement to the nurses' verbal instructions.

Throughout the booklet there are clues to the parents on what kind of response to make to the child in various situations. There is also a short discussion of what the child's behavior may be after returning home and a suggestion that the parent may want to consult the doctor if the behavior is disturbing. From this introduction, the child and his family begin to become familiar with the pediatric services as a whole.

The wards for those children 3 to 10 years old and teenagers have been planned with the nursing station as the central core; the rooms on both sides open toward the station, and the space between, more a general area than a hallway, is used by parents, ambulatory children, and the staff. The windows and doors of the rooms are decorated with pictures made by the children and appropriate decorations put there by the staff. There are playrooms for different ages, and near the entrance of the unit is a large lounge for parents with a television, a telephone, and one of the wall-unit beds that are a feature of the division. These beds, which fold down from the walls and become an unobtrusive wooden panel when not in use, have mattresses and a self-contained light. Bedding is brought by the nurses for parents who wish to stay overnight. A notice on the panel informs parents that the bed is for their use without charge and gives appropriate instructions.

The nurseries for special and premature babies contain 22

cribs and take infants up to 2 months old. As in the rest
of pediatrics visiting hours are open to parents, and mothers
not only visit but hold and feed their premature babies
whenever possible. Parents can telephone to find out the
condition of their babies at any time, day or night. There are
rocking chairs for parents. No masks are required unless the
child is in isolation; masks were discarded more than five
years ago, and there has been no rise in infections or
contagion on the ward. The nurses do a good deal of teaching
and counseling as the mothers learn to care for their children.
The same informality that pervades the pediatric floors is
found here—a toy tied to a crib; a sleeping premature infant
in an embroidered yellow dress, ready to go home within the
half-hour; a little green suit on a hanger at the end of the
crib, waiting for the tiny boy sleeping there.

A group meeting for parents of the premature babies is
held every Monday evening for informal discussion of the
problems of caring for the babies at home. Originated by two
graduate nursing students, it was endorsed by the medical
and nursing staffs. At first the doctors were somewhat
concerned that the students would find the group tending to
become a "group therapy" session and beyond their abilities
to handle; however, a plan was evolved under which the
group meeting would be initiated by the graduate students
and then be taken over by the nursing staff. At first the
initiators sent out letters to parents, but they soon found
that the most effective way of publicizing the meetings was
to wait in the premature babies wards and invite the parents
personally, informally aided by a posted sign showing the
place and time of the meetings.

As the meetings were gradually taken over by the nursing
staff, two of whom conduct them on off-duty hours,
students still sat in to effect an easy transition. Meetings have
now changed character somewhat from the original informal

airing of questions and fears, being structured more around specific information. While Miss Carol Garrett, the head nurse, will say that the best and most useful help for parents of babies who are premature or have birth defects is still one-to-one counseling, she thinks that groups can also be helpful, particularly when the staff's time is limited. "The nurses have the opportunity to pick up many clues to the parents' stresses and feelings," she says. "They may want to go on with such meetings for mutual benefit even if we can make the time and opportunity for one-to-one counseling as well." Miss Susan Varner, the social worker for this unit, also finds the group helpful, since the leaders may be able to refer to her mothers whom they feel need more specialized help. "For instance, an unwed mother who is taking part in the group can participate without giving any information as to her status, and then we can help her as well with her particular problems of being a single parent. Or the group leaders may want to consult us about how to present a particular problem, even though we are not participants in the group. Then we share information with them, so that they can be careful in difficult areas."

Social work and nursing have a close and mutually supportive relationship in this unit, as is true generally of all the disciplines in pediatrics at the Medical Center. One of the most forward-looking aspects of social work at the hospital is that being carried on with "high-risk" parents, those with potential problems centering about the child. Miss Varner, in addition to being the social worker for the premature babies nursery, also works with high-risk parents and with families of multidefective babies. She describes this role as follows.

Here at the hospital we have been very interested in doing preventive work with mothers, particularly with those women in the child-bearing years who are going to be having more babies in the future. We do not work with the babies; the mothers are our concern. We start through the obstetrical and gynecological services, trying to do counseling with the women during pregnancy, to assess their ability to be parents, and to help them before problems become acute. For instance, with a parent whom we feel may be a potential child-batterer, we try to do counseling during pregnancy and make resources available to her to prevent later child-battering or child neglect. The unwed mother, particularly if she is very young, is potentially a mother with problems—she may not be eating properly, she may be living on very limited funds, she may not know what her feelings about the baby really are. Diabetic mothers may be high-risk mothers; so may mothers from deprived areas with extremely large families.

We use public health nurses and community social workers out in the field until the baby is discharged. We hope that the parents—the mother, if not both—can be persuaded to come and spend a good deal of time here in the three or four days before the child is discharged, so that they can learn total care of the infant with the help of the staff, particularly if they are frightened. We have funds through the social service department for fares and housing. With low-income parents who will perhaps be having other children, we want to avoid penalizing their whole family because of one child. For the same reason, we make them aware that birth control counseling is available. Parents who have a child with multiple birth defects—particularly if it is the first child—are often in a state of shock, sorrow, and dread. Until they are able to cope with their own feelings, it is often a relief to them to know that they need not have other children unless they choose to.

Four of us see more than five hundred people a year. We see a mother all during her pregnancy if possible, and through delivery, an eleven-month coverage. We continue following her after that if she has the need and if we have come to know her so well that it would be harmful to break off the relationship. We refer some mothers to other agencies; with some, we will perhaps keep in touch for three or four years.

We also have, in addition to our regular caseload, patients whom we have never seen before who come to have their babies and then disappear again. In a year we may have eight or nine hundred of these. One of the most compelling reasons for this kind of early preventive work with parents is clear when, as a social worker, you are involved in work with adolescents. I have seen difficult problems that could have been helped or prevented if strains and difficulties had been dealt with in the earliest stages—when the parents were expecting the child, or when he was an infant. Problems between parents and children can be exacerbated by the time the child is an adolescent until it is almost too late to solve them. Problems can multiply with siblings in the family and can snowball if they are not helped in time.

I feel that it is important to work with the husbands. We are hoping to involve them more than we do now.

We find that our informal work with the nurses on the ward is very valuable. We can indicate to them what signs to watch for, and they are invaluable about letting us know when there are signs of stress. A mother who is frightened of feeding or touching her baby, for instance—a nurse can see this much more quickly than we can. Then we can help the mother. The more alert we are to danger signals, the more later problems we may be able to help prevent.

The social workers consult with the doctors in a weekly case conference. Consultations with the nurses are usually held informally on the wards. There are two social workers for obstetrics who see the normal newborns; one of them will sometimes follow an infant with a birth defect or a premature baby because she knows the mother well and wants to keep up the ongoing relationship.

Miss Varner sees a close interaction between nursing and social service as vital to the overall care of the patient. "I know I could not work effectively without the nurses' help," she says, "and I think that without me they would be less able to deal with the many emotional problems that affect the patient." She sees the greatest problem in interdepartmental communication to be the time factor—the lack of time to sit down and talk over problems and the fitting of decisions and information into the busy schedules of doctors, surgeons, and staff slow some of the steps that could be taken to solve problems. Funds for housing out-of-town parents so that the family can be involved in the child's care are another great need. There are funds, but they never reach quite far enough—to her regret.

Even with these problems, the communication between departments is good and crosses traditional lines. Miss Harriet Walker, supervisor of pediatric social work for patients up to 18 years old, shares information with Miss Varner, and they sometimes follow patients or parents in each other's department to assure continuity of care. Communication with outside agencies, public health nurses in particular, is also good. Often the social work department is in touch with a public health nurse while the baby and mother are still in the hospital to be sure that the problems of the family can be solved before the new baby is brought home.

The social workers draw on the resources of doctors, nurses, an intern in psychology, the consultant services of four psychiatric fellows who are assigned to various wards, and use the treatment clinic at the psychiatric hospital of the Medical Center. They also use and communicate with many outside community facilities, presenting cases and trying to keep avenues of communication strong among all the services involved with the family.

Twenty-eight Foster Grandparents, funded by the Office

of Economic Opportunity (O.E.O.), now work in the pediatric division in three shifts; at one time there were forty, and many of the staff would welcome that number again. (The number was reduced when O.E.O. funds were cut.) A dramatic instance of the usefulness of these paid workers is quoted: "We had one baby whose medical tests showed that there was no organic problem, but at 18 months he was small and developmentally only 3 months old, and he never smiled. The doctor ordered 'Foster Grandmothers around the clock.' That meant three Grandmothers in shifts. Only three days later the baby had gained two pounds and progressed developmentally to the 6-month level. It was hard to believe. He was just a different child."

Miss Walker stresses that in the working relationship between the department of social work and the doctors, medical and socioeconomic aspects of every case must be fully shared in order to assure really comprehensive care of the child. One new development has been made that she considers extremely valuable: "Dr. Kempe has added some requirements for internship here, and greater stress is laid on the applicant's attitude toward total patient care. This screening has made the change even more noticeable this year."

The social service department also has an orientation course and in-service training for the nursing staff. Miss Walker's office is adjacent to the pediatric units, and she spends a good deal of time on the wards in consultation with the nurses and the families. "Some families are not sure what a social worker does," she says. "They think it has something to do with public assistance or welfare. We try to explain what they can use us for. We tell them that the doctor and nurses are taking care of the child, but that sometimes there are family problems that are important too, and we are here to help with those. They may be skeptical at first."

Communication and cooperation are the basic tenets of this department's philosophy. "We're all contributing to the patient and the family, and to each other's jobs. No one person is alone with a problem—we're all important."

The Intensive Therapy Unit allows a great deal of participation by parents. They not infrequently carry out some medical procedures for their children such as postural drainage, tracheal suction, changing burn dressings, and so on. There are 2 rooms for overnight stay by parents whose children are in the Intensive Therapy Unit.

"It doesn't make our work easier to have the parents," says Mary Sue Jack, the assistant head nurse, "but it is more rewarding. Pediatric nursing is really 75 percent parents—they're so much better for the child. We don't encourage many visitors here, but parents are different. In many ways they become our patients too."

One of the difficulties for a nurse in the Intensive Therapy Unit is that during her initial weeks in the unit she may feel inadequate about her ability to deal with the parent of a critically ill child. This is gradually overcome as she becomes more sure of herself and as she realizes how much the parents need her support. Many parents who have led active lives find themselves without any occupation to relieve the tension over long hours and sometimes many days. The nursing staff in the Intensive Therapy Unit feels that parents are more able to cope with the child's illness and their own feelings if they can be encouraged to feel that they are making a contribution.

For instance, the mother of a child who had suffered a head injury and had been comatose for two months was taught how to encourage the child by talking to him in a way that did not put a burden of response on him. She was also coached in giving him a limited range of motion and later in how to feed him from a feeding tube. When the child began to respond, the mother had the reward and satisfaction of feeling that she had been instrumental in his progress instead of being a helpless outsider.

Occasionally a mother who has particular strength in relating to others will be encouraged to talk to another mother who feels lonely or has lost hope. Parents may like to reminisce about the child when he was well, and airing their feelings to each other is a good outlet. However, one real problem with parents of a critically ill child is their tendency to stay to the point of exhaustion, and tact and firmness are sometimes needed to convince a parent to go home for a rest or to spend some time away from the unit. There are parents whose anxieties become too difficult for the nursing staff to handle or who upset the others in the unit. When this happens, the staff can call upon a hospital psychiatrist for consultation. The nurses can also turn to the authority of the doctor on the case, who can usually convince the parent of the realities involved. At present, a monthly nursing staff consultation with the psychiatrist is being tried experimentally on a scheduled basis. Parents are invited and encouraged to come in before the child's surgery, and there is preoperative orientation for the child and parent. Routinely, when a parent and child are being transferred from the Intensive Therapy Unit to the pediatric ward, there is an attempt to have them visit the ward to see the new surroundings and meet the nurses. Sometimes a child to be transferred to the Intensive Therapy Unit from general pediatrics comes for a visit, for instance, a child scheduled for cardiac surgery. The nurses on the Intensive Therapy Unit show the parent and child as much as they think will be informative and helpful without appearing frightening.

Miss Jack thinks that this intercommunication is very

valuable to the nursing staff as well as to the children and parents. She would like to see it given even more emphasis, since a child changing locations often resists new ways of doing things. Parents are also sometimes slow to understand the routines in the new place as opposed to the familiar routines they have just left.

One of the very difficult problems for the staff in this unit is dealing with the family of a dying child. They have found that there is a tendency in many cases for the family to move away from the child in their grief at the anticipation of death, and the nurses sometimes find in themselves a tendency to avoid the parents at this time because they feel they may be intruding. Actually, this may be the time when their support for the parent would be most helpful. Thus in the nurses' orientation here, stress is laid on talking to parents and allowing them to talk. "Look at the parents. Don't avoid them or ignore the fact that they are there," is one of the underlying themes of the unit. When these children are the donors of a liver or kidney for transplantation, the staff finds that one successful way of giving comfort and support is to interest the parents in the child-recipient of the transplant. Some parents have visited these children after the death of their own and have taken some comfort from the fact that a child is benefiting, although they themselves are bereaved. Others will telephone inquiries on the condition of the recipient.

It is not unusual for parents to send toys or a letter to the unit after the death of a child, in gratitude for having been able to share in his care and comfort. Sometimes even those parents who seemed least responsive to the efforts of the staff to support them through the ordeal will later express their thanks.

An additional complication on this unit is dealing with

parents and children when an emergency arises. One of the most difficult of these is an acute cardiac arrest, and the nurses follow an emergency plan for all parents and patients as well as for the child involved, as Miss Jack explains.

One of us always goes around quickly to the parents who are with their children while the others are busy with the patient and asks them if they will go outside. We ask them to go immediately because we have an emergency; we'll tell them as soon as they can come back into the unit. This is because what they can hear will be very upsetting to them, and they may misinterpret what we are doing. They are always very understanding, and they leave. The same nurse tries to reassure and screen off the children—and that's harder if they can hear and be worried. We let them know that we will talk to them after the emergency.

There are very few occasions when we have to do this, with no time to explain. But when we do, we've always found the parents very cooperative. I think on the whole they've learned to trust us, and they know we're just trying to do the best for their children. Sometimes a mother will ask us to tell her child if another child has died because she doesn't feel she can do it. We try to encourage her to let the child talk about it and to listen. We'd rather tell the child in her presence and help both communicate with each other.

Social workers help the staff of the Intensive Therapy Unit by dealing with the parents' problems of where to stay near the hospital, financial help if needed, transportation, emotional support, and help with problems at home. The transplant team has its own social worker who can give help to the particular families involved. On occasion a Foster Grandparent has been used to emotionally support a child who needed extra care.

"I think it's a harder and more demanding job than working in a unit of this kind in which parents are not allowed to take part," says Miss Jack. "We all feel so bad when we lose a child, for instance. But if we think that we've helped the family to go on and if we can see that our help and friendship have made it easier for the mother, then we see that our work has another dimension of value and we know that we've done something positive, despite the tragedy."

On the whole, nurses are aware before they come to work at the University of Colorado Medical Center that this is the prevailing atmosphere. They come because they are in sympathy with it. But responsibility for the ongoing and dynamic approach to total child care lies with the department heads and other members of the staff, who are constantly evaluating the daily procedures and searching for ways to make things better. Dr. Henry Silver gives the key to the program.

We are a state institution and we cannot and do not want to go out and solicit funds. Much of what we do doesn't cost money. Dr. Kempe and I ask ourselves, "What is it we are doing so badly that we'd better improve it in a hurry?" You can always see something right away that needs improving, and then you try to figure out the simplest way of making the change. We work on the assumption that everybody cares—the nurses, the residents, the social workers, the parents. Everyone does want to do what is best for the children.

It's difficult to ask the parents whether they like this or that and what should be changed, since they believe, of course, that they have brought their child to a place where he will get the best possible care. So they really can't question visiting hours. If you told them they could only come for one hour a week, they could only assume that you know what is best.

If you assume that everyone really cares—and we do believe that—then, even if it will be inconvenient to change, everyone will put up with it. Of course, change is always threatening—any change—so we consult everyone involved; but we don't say, "Do you want to do this?" Rather we say, "How shall we go about doing this?" All we want to do is make children more comfortable on a ward. When we think of something, we try to do it.

We have an unusual hospital administrator. His attitude is always one of really wanting to implement the things we want to do. He has to set financial limitations, and we recognize that, but we know that he is primarily interested in making this a better hospital for the patients and a better job for us—not in maintaining the status quo.

The child is the focus. We want to improve not only his health care, but every aspect of his life. When there is a mother who doesn't come to see a child here who needs her, it's our business to find out what the problem is at home. Perhaps she has a large family she can't leave; perhaps it's really impossible for her to come. Then we have to be very sure that we can give this child a parent surrogate to fill in for her and give him what he needs. We can see some indications that everyone feels better about doing things the way we do; for instance, the children cry less. With limited visiting hours there's a great deal of crying sometimes because the children are reproaching their parents, "Why didn't you come before this?" and "Why do you have to go away now?" But with open hours the children can understand the explanations— that a mother has to go home and take care of the family; that a father must go to his job.

It seems to us that some of the changes have made the parents feel more at ease, and therefore they can often be very helpful to the nurses. The nurses get more rewards from the job—it's more interesting. And the children seem to be happier. You can't measure these things on charts and graphs. We don't have any particular statistics on many of these things we do, but they work.

There are many more ways in which we would like to expand our services. For one thing, we would like more outreach into the community. Our patients come from a large area, and we'd like to have more interaction with the rural areas.

The final word on pediatrics at the University of Colorado Medical Center is summed up in the conviction of Dr. Henry Kempe and Dr. Silver that is the keynote of their innovations and their program: "Nothing really frightens us about change. If we can see that a change may be useful, if we can see that it could make things easier, we're never afraid to try it."

REFERENCES

Bright, F. The pediatric nurse and parental anxiety. *Nursing Forum* 4:30-47, 1965.

Bright, F. Parental Anxiety—A Barrier to Communication. *Proceedings of the American Nursing Association Clinical Sessions, 1966.* Pp. 13-20.

Haller, J., Talbert, J. L., and Dombro, R. H. *The Hospitalized Child and His Family.* Baltimore: The Johns Hopkins Press, 1967.

Pickett, L. The hospital environment for the pediatric surgical patient. *Pediatric Clinics of North America* 16:530-542, 1969.

Prugh, D. G., Staub, E. M., Sands, H. H., Kirschbaum, R. M., and Lenihan, E. A. A study of the emotional reactions of children and families to hospitalization and illness. *American Journal of Orthopsychiatry* 23:70-106, 1953.

Robertson, J. *Hospitals and Children: A Parent's Eye View.* New York: International Universities Press, 1964.

Rosen, V. H. The role of denial in acute post-operative affective reactions following removal of body parts. *Psychosomatic Medicine* 12:6, 1960.

Rothman, P. E. A note on hospitalization. *Pediatrics* 30:995-998, 1962.

Wolf, R. E. The Hospital and the Child. In A. Solnit and S. Provence (Eds.), *Modern Perspectives in Child Development.* New York: International Universities Press, 1963. Pp. 409-418.

Woodward, J. Emotional disturbances of burned children. *British Medical Journal* 1:1009-1013, 1959.

4

New Approaches in Old Facilities

THE University of Colorado Medical Center in Denver and The Johns Hopkins Hospital in Baltimore are fortunate in the planning and construction that went into their accommodations for parents. The medical staff and administration of both hospitals were concerned with the need for keeping parents with their children, and this concern influenced the new construction from its initial stages. Two other hospitals exclusively for children are now in a similar prebuilding period. The Children's Hospital of Philadelphia and Babies and Childrens Hospital of Cleveland will both be housed in larger facilities in the near future, and both are already committed to a policy of parent involvement, although at present their space is limited.

At the time of this study both these hospitals were in old buildings, with services that had outgrown their facilities, although Babies and Childrens Hospital has now moved into its new building. Both are teaching hospitals, taking patients from their immediate vicinity and from considerable distances, and both are carrying out intensive research programs. Both have urban locations: Children's Hospital of Philadelphia is in the heart of a low-income neighborhood that is served by its clinics, and Babies and Childrens Hospital is part of a large complex, University Hospitals of Cleveland, within the city.

Inside these hospitals there are similar small elevators inadequate for the traffic burden they carry, but despite the inconveniences of outdated architectural construction there is an atmosphere of freedom and openness. This is an indefinable quality in a hospital, particularly in one in which hallways are apt to be confusing and always crowded. What is most noticeable perhaps is the absence of a forbidding atmosphere rather than something that is actually present. The feeling prevails that there are no barriers to entering any given section, a general emphasis on making personal contact rather than showing a pass made out at the desk. Although there are regulations and limitations on certain areas and hours, these are less emphasized than the right of families to be present. The overall atmosphere in both hospitals can only be described in the word *reasonable,* a reasonable request from a parent being considered on its own merits rather than in reference to set rules.

An example of the spirit in which hospitalization is carried out is seen on one of the wards at Children's Hospital of Philadelphia; a sink in the ward that is too high for 3- and 4-year-olds to reach from the floor has a set of steps built up to it. An enthusiastic little boy of 3 with a random handful of plastic dishes climbs the steps himself, turns the water on to a satisfactory splash, and busily washes his dishes, with no word of reproof from the child activities worker, the nurse, or the two mothers nearby. The elementary precaution of dressing him in a plastic apron had been taken care of, and he was in complete charge of the project. The staff here obviously prefers play, which is a release for the child, to a floor that is kept shining.

This kind of incident is observable daily in both hospitals in many different ways. In both, the nursing department is active in setting the tone of friendliness toward parents and informality with the children. This is not an unthinking or indifferent policy, but a part of in-service training and a constant example of what the role of nursing should be. At The Johns Hopkins Hospital and at the University of Colorado Medical Center, much of the impetus for changes in approach came from the medical heads of departments and faculties. At Children's Hospital of Philadelphia and Babies and Childrens Hospital, some of the pioneering in new methods and new understanding has stemmed directly from the efforts of the departments of nursing, which in both places have widely influenced the tone of the hospital.

CHILDREN'S HOSPITAL OF PHILADELPHIA

Children's Hospital of Philadelphia, founded in 1855, is the first and oldest hospital exclusively for children in the United States. Housed in an impressive but old-fashioned building, it is currently constructing a comprehensive new hospital and Child Guidance Center. It is presently located in the heart of a low-income neighborhood; one of its out-patient clinics, Operation Rebound, centers on the involvement and ongoing care of entire families who live within an easy distance of the hospital. In this it is similar to a comparable clinic program at The Johns Hopkins Hospital, serving "corridors" of families in the area surrounding the hospital itself. (These two programs are discussed further in Chapter 6.)

Children's Hospital of Philadelphia welcomes parents at any time and allows rooming in, although its facilities are limited. The admission booklet tells parents in a somewhat discouraging way: "Rooming in for mothers is available in a few rooms. Mothers must be up and dressed at 7:30 A.M. Meals are not served to parents staying with their child . . ." In fact, however, the hospital encourages and helps mothers stay with short-term surgical patients, such as those who are having a tonsillectomy or a hernia operation. It is also very supportive of parents with children in the Intensive Care Unit, those with cardiac problems, and other special patients.

Like Boston Floating Hospital, Children's Hospital of Philadelphia was encouraged in its involvement of parents by its play program. Started in the first year of the hospital's existence by a Board of Lady Visitors a program to "entertain and educate the hospitalized child" was very successful. This program did not involve parents with the children, but it was one of the earliest in the country to recognize the importance of play as an outlet for children under stress, and it has moved in various stages toward a very complete program that eventually included education of the staff and interaction with parents. Now it has compiled sheets of staff instructions covering almost every nonmedical aspect of child care, and these facilitate communication between departments as well as the training of child activities workers and nurses. For instance, the social work department has a very comprehensive and concise sheet of instructions for nurses to use in identifying patients who may need their services. Their suggested criteria are divided into two sections: under *Parents,* some of the signs to watch for are: (1) mothers under 18 years old; (2) a person admitting the child who is not a responsible relative; and (3) a parent who is a poor historian on the recent history of the presenting illness (confused, lack of recall, changes in history); under *Child:* (1) all ingestions; (2) all burns; (3) head injuries of unclear origin in a child under age 2; and (4) a child showing signs of abuse and/or neglect, and so forth. There are also a series of general suggestions about families needing such concrete services as transportation, drugs, or orthopedic appliances.

The Children's Activities Program was established in its present form in 1951 and is supported through the Junior League of Philadelphia. Under its Coordinator, Miss Mary M. Brooks, are four full-time professional child-care workers and two part-time male workers who are preprofessional college students. Student nurses are assigned to the program for a full week to further their understanding of children. The Children's Activities Program here has strong support from the medical and nursing staff. This helps to make its activities very effective. The coordinator of this program is accepted as a full member of the team in the overall care of the children.

In an article for the journal of the National Association of Nursery Education, Miss Brooks gives her philosophy and that of the hospital staff.[1] She writes in part:

... This is a family-centered hospital, seeking ways to help children face hospitalization without undue trauma. Always of major importance is the fact that these services are to help the child and his family, not to replace parents or serve as a substitute for them. We constantly try to emphasize that neither anyone nor anything can or should serve as a substitute parent for the hospitalized child. Every effort is made to encourage parents to visit as often as possible,

---

[1]Brooks, M. Constructive play experiences for the hospitalized child. *Journal of Nursery Education* 12:9, 1957.

preferably each day, and to stay as long as possible . . . From the study of child development and observation of children in the hospital it is clear that fear of desertion by the parents is very strong . . . Usually every child who can possibly go home for Christmas Day is allowed to do so, even if it means returning the next day. Elective admissions are not planned for the week just preceding Christmas . . .

In 1964 Miss E. Cleves Rothrock, director of nursing, conceived the idea of a single department in the hospital responsible for helping parents become a part of the total health team caring for their children, a program which has since been studied as a model by other hospitals. (The Children's Hospital Medical Center of Boston has staffed a position entitled Coordinator of Parent Education, based on the prototype position at Children's Hospital of Philadelphia held by Mrs. Edith Amend, R.N.)

Mrs. Amend's duties as Coordinator of Parent Education cover a wide range of activities. She counsels parents both individually and in groups. She prepares teaching guides for the nursing staff and serves as a buffer between the parent, the doctor, and the nurses. In addition, she conducts period surveys and studies in specific aspects of child care and works closely with the Children's Activities Program and the social service department.

A regularly scheduled part of her day is the morning group conference with children scheduled for ear, nose, and throat surgery (usually tonsillectomies) who are accompanied by their parents. In a pleasant conference room with a large center table there are coloring books and crayons as a gift from the hospital to the children. Mrs. Amend is not in uniform, and the session is highly informal. When everyone is comfortably settled at the table, Mrs. Amend explains to the children the entire procedure that will take place. She uses first names and pauses often for questions. While the children sometimes appear to be busy with their coloring books and paying little or no attention, she believes that they have amazing recall of the information she has given them. The parents hear everything that is said to the children and sometimes intervene to prompt the children to comment or to add information.

Mrs. Amend starts by outlining in exact sequence what the child will do and see from the time he leaves the conference room—who will be upstairs, what it will look like, and what he can expect. She then moves on to the preparation for surgery, how the child will feel, and what to expect on waking from the anesthetic. "And after you've been dreaming, who will be the very first person you'll see when you open your eyes? Not me—you won't want to see me! And not the doctor. You'll see Mommy, of course. She'll be right there beside you, and she'll stay all night with you, so if you wake up you can just look over and see that she's there."

About the operation she is specific and reassuring. To a child scheduled for a tonsillectomy: "Do you know where your tonsils are? Mommy told you, didn't she? Where are they? That's right. They're right here. And we take them out like this: we open your mouth, and we just go right in there and take them out. Through your mouth. And that's the only part of you we touch when you're asleep. We don't touch anything else at all."

When she has completed giving information to the child, with many chances to elicit questions interspersed with casual references to the child as an individual—home, siblings, pets, and toys—Mrs. Amend tells the children, "Now I'm going to tell your mother what will happen to her in the hospital, but you listen, because there aren't any secrets from you. You'll know everything I tell her and everything she's going to do while you're here."

With the mother she uses more sophisticated terms and

describes the procedures, the length of time that the child will probably be in surgery, and the suggested ways in which a parent can help. "Then, while she's in surgery, it would be a good idea for you to go and get some lunch. There will probably be about a four-hour wait; she'll be two or three hours in the recovery room. She knows you'll be there when she wakes up. We'll let you know in plenty of time. That's the important thing—that you be right by her as soon as she opens her eyes."

From this she moves on to discuss the details of spending the night, the refrigerator on the ward from which the mother can get the child ice cream or Popsicles at any time, the importance of frequent sips of a liquid, financial arrangements, and even parking facilities. She also tells the mother exactly how long to stay after the preoperative sedation is given (five minutes) and why she should leave then. When she is satisfied that both mother and child are fully informed and their questions answered, she directs them upstairs, assures them that she will see them later on the ward, and telephones the ward staff to say that they are on the way.

Mrs. Amend consults with the anesthesiologist about the families to give him clues for approaching each individual. He makes an early visit to each child on the ward to familiarize the child with his face before they meet in the operating room, where he will be masked. On the ward he explains to the child that under the unfamiliar mask will be his friendly face and that the child will recognize his voice. Often the child is also reassured to know that he himself will be recognized by the anesthesiologist.

Unlike many hospitals, Children's Hospital of Philadelphia takes short-term stays very seriously and treats tonsillectomies as major surgery. It is felt that such patients are often ill prepared and are not reassured about the situation by either staff or parents because it is assumed that the experience is short and will soon be forgotten. "But it is often harder and more traumatic for the children. They come in perfectly well, have a strange and painful experience here, and then go out feeling terrible—they have no way of knowing what to expect. Mothers often want to cling to the child, interfering with the sedation. Now we let them know what to expect, why we want them to wait and where, and it's much easier for them."

Mrs. Amend also works with hernia patients. She sees all the patients undergoing heart surgery and cardiac catheterization, particularly babies and newborns, in order to counsel their parents more effectively. She counsels the parents of critically or terminally ill children in the Intensive Care Unit. Referrals come to her from doctors, department supervisors, and staff nurses. "But there's only one of me, and sometimes there just isn't time to do as much as I'd like," she says ruefully.

She has also carried out a study on the preparation of children for surgery. Her findings showed that in a group of children prepared ahead of time, the anxiety level rose just after the preparation, but following surgery the anxiety had gone down noticeably. A follow-up study six weeks later showed very little anxiety in this group. In contrast, a control group of children, who were not prepared at all, showed less anxiety until they were given preoperative injections on the ward, at which time their anxiety rose sharply. A follow-up study six weeks later showed that there was still a high anxiety level. Although the groups tested were comparatively small, the staff feels that the indications for preparation of both mother and child are unmistakable.

Patients in for cardiac catheterization are sent a booklet

before admission, *Michael's Heart Test,* while those in for heart surgery get *Margaret's Heart Operation.*[2] Both booklets are illustrated with step-by-step photographs of children undergoing the hospital procedures, and the accompanying text describes clearly what the patient will experience. Photographs of the cardiac catheterization laboratory show in detail the unfamiliar equipment used for the operation so both parent and child will be acquainted with the machines and procedure. After admission of surgical patients, the parent and child together are given a tour of the Intensive Care Unit. Miss Brooks and her staff help to prepare children for catheterization, one example of how the Children's Activities staff and the nursing staff cooperate.

The mother of one cardiac patient summed up her feelings: "It wasn't frightening to me to see her in the Intensive Care Unit. We had had a tour the day before so I knew what it was like there. And then we'd read the Margaret book at home. She's been fine. She wasn't smiling, you know, but she was just taking it all in. She likes the hospital. The nurses are nice, you know. Friendly."

"And they don't mention anything about bed-wetting or mistakes," added the nearby mother of a 4-year-old. "You can ask them questions like, 'Why is my child in a mist tent?' They're, well, sincere."

These mothers were tired and the area was busy, but the children moved back and forth between the play materials and their mothers with ease. They seemed to have no apprehension about doctors and nurses who came by or strangers on the unit.

---

[2]Children's Hospital of Philadelphia. *Margaret's Heart Operation* and *Michael's Heart Test.* Philadelphia: Public Relations Department, Children's Hospital of Philadelphia.

Children with Leukemia

Parents whose children have leukemia get special help and counseling from Dr. Charles Koch, consultant to the hospital from the Child Guidance Clinic of the University of Pennsylvania. A psychiatrist, Dr. Koch's special concern is the emotional well-being of a child with this disease in the context of his total surroundings, and his regular weekly meetings with all the staff set up joint goals for both the child and the family.

There is a file at the nurses' station in which notes about the patient and his parents are made by staff members so that all of them are kept informed about special indications even through changing shifts; it is kept at the desk by the medical charts so it is readily available.

Besides meeting with the staff, Dr. Koch holds group meetings for parents of children with leukemia and also does individual counseling. He tries to make sure that every newly admitted patient and his family have some personal help, either from himself or from a staff member. He is equally concerned with the feelings of the nurses who care for these terminally ill patients. He feels that one advantage of the team approach to such care is that there can be relief for individual nurses from the strain of involvement, and that understanding and insight can ease some of the anxieties and stress.

Crisis, says Dr. Koch, can be a maturing experience, and intervention by a skilled professional in a situation which overwhelms a family is an important part of dealing with crisis. A crisis he defines as something which makes changes in feelings, during which perhaps there is a surfacing of elements which were not previously understood and which give an opportunity for building strength. It is his aim that both staff and parents be encouraged to make use of their concern and skills in positive ways.

In addition to the weekly staff conference with Dr. Koch, there is a daily nursing conference on the floor dealing with the medical treatment, the child's feelings and activities, and the involvement of parents in caring for their children. One gain which has resulted from these conferences is that nurses are increasingly aware of the positive contribution they are making to the future strength and well-being of entire families. Formerly, there had sometimes been difficulty in keeping the unit adequately staffed, but now staffing is less of a problem; nurses have sometimes even requested duty in this unit because they find working with families to be rewarding.

Departmental Relationships

The close working relationship between departments and the mutual respect of various disciplines is evident at Children's Hospital of Philadelphia. Dr. Henry Cecil, who is in charge of the training program for residents, stresses communication between professionals and between parents and those who care for the child. "We try," he says, "to teach counseling, interviewing, and child development, in seminars and individually. A lot of people go into medicine interested only in the scientific aspects and feel that they should remain impersonal. Parents are often looked upon as nuisances. If you are a busy professional, you don't want to bother with them, although actually the mother needs a great deal more attention in times of stress, not less. But medicine is a rapidly changing service. If we could present to the applicant a more realistic picture of his profession, we might get a more appropriate person, at least from the point of view of patient care. We need the scientific person, but we need the patient-care person, too. In many ways, nursing has done a better job of that kind of teaching than we have in medicine."

Certainly Children's Hospital of Philadelphia has a department of nursing that, under the direction of Miss Rothrock, is very much aware of and responsive to the needs of families. On one occasion, for instance, a mother who was giving excellent care to her infant in the hospital found that her 3-year-old at home was feeling abandoned and neglected. The whole family visited together in the hospital for several days so that the 3-year-old could see what his mother was doing and be reassured that they were still a united family.

Miss Rothrock points out a particular benefit of open visiting hours that she feels is important. Since there are no limits, day or night, to visiting in this hospital, parents may, and occasionally have, come in at midnight or at four o'clock in the morning. "The message that comes through to them, particularly if they are very anxious parents, is that no harm is being done to the child. This communication builds trust in the hospital and the staff. Certainly, this makes it easier to explain what we are doing and why."

Two aspects of this hospital are particularly impressive: the good communication among various disciplines and the informality and genuine ease of children and parents, even in facilities which have become overcrowded.

In the 10-bed units in which children of various ages are housed, the center of the ward is an informal playroom. Around the table may be children who are ambulatory or perhaps in wheelchairs. The beds of those on bed rest are pulled near the center so that those children too can take a limited part in the activities. In one such ward, a play specialist is supervising several children at the table, a little girl with a small tub of water is washing doll clothes and hanging them on a line rigged up between two beds, two mothers are watching the play, and a nurse pauses to admire one child's crayon drawing and exchange a few words with a mother. Here are patients, mothers, play activities staff, and nursing staff all aware of and communicating with each other, with no division of area or spheres of authority. Miss Brooks feels that there is great benefit in having the play directly centered in the unit. Although a child may be interrupted in what he is doing for medication or for a visit from the doctor, he can carry on his activities with more continuity and less resentment if he does not have to leave the area. Children who are confined to bed feel less deprived since they can be a part of the activity on the ward and do not have to feel left out while others have special privileges.

Upstairs in another unit, children are making candy apples around a table in the hall next to the wards. Again, they are supervised by a member of the children's activities department. A nurse, carefully carrying off a candy apple in waxed paper, was being watched closely by one small boy.

"I'm saving it for him," she explained. "He made it and it looks so good, but he can't eat it today. We'll ask the doctor, and maybe he can have it tomorrow."

Candy apples dripping caramel, tubs of water, clay, and a 3-year-old climbing a set of steps to get at a fixed washbasin and turn on the faucets are all surprisingly homelike and messy activities to find in a hospital ward. Apparently the children's enjoyment of these activities in this atmosphere is taken for granted and enjoyed by the nursing staff.

Space limitations at the hospital can cause frustration, although some of these problems will be eased by the new building currently under construction. But there is an intangible feeling here: busy, crowded, sometimes noisy as it is, Children's Hospital of Philadelphia gives the feeling not of being an institution for the diagnosis of disease and curing of symptoms, but of being a place where human beings are concerned with the care and well-being of everybody's children.

BABIES AND CHILDRENS HOSPITAL OF CLEVELAND

Babies and Childrens Hospital of the University Hospitals of Cleveland has two programs primarily and specifically geared to meet the psychological needs of children and their parents while the children are ill and hospitalized. One of these is the Child Life Program, and the other is the Family-Centered Care Program. The major assumption on which both rest is that attention focused on psychological needs when the child is in the hospital will prevent emotional sequelae. The purpose of this section is to describe the development and conduct of the Family-Centered Care Program.

In a large complex of university hospitals, Babies and Childrens Hospital was housed in an old-fashioned, somewhat forbidding building; the interior seemed shabby and crowded, inconvenient but friendly. In late summer of 1971, a new and expanded hospital became ready for occupancy.

In the old building there were roll-away beds and reclining chairs for parents who stayed overnight and a limited number of rooms for a mother and child rooming together. The new building allows for about 20 percent rooming in.

When it is known in advance that a child will be admitted, parents are sent a beautifully designed booklet about the hospital illustrated with drawings made by previously hospitalized children. It invites the parents and child, if appropriate, to participate in one of the weekly preadmission tours, conducted by the senior clinical nurses, which give them an opportunity to ask questions. This is one of the few hospitals with such tours, and the booklet supplies a telephone number the parents can call to make arrangements. It also indicates that professional personnel are available to help the mother cope with emotional responses to the hospitalization with which she desires assistance. One page is headed, "How You Can Help in the Hospital."

Both you and your child can benefit from your participation in his hospital care. We encourage you to help with routine bathing, dressing and feeding of your child, especially if he is in the infant or preschool age group. Please make arrangements for this with the nurse in charge.

You may help your child with school lessons, play games with him, or read to him. Space permitting, one parent may sleep at the hospital if it is considered advisable by the medical and nursing staffs. Please discuss your plans for overnight stay with the nurse in charge.

The booklet also suggests that parents leave siblings at home to allow the child-patient their undivided attention for several hours on the day he is admitted. In the section on surgery the booklet specifies that the mother may accompany the child to the elevators of the building in which the surgery is done, that she will be told where to wait to see the doctor after surgery, and that she may stay with the child for the rest of the day after surgery. Other information in the booklet gives visiting hours—unrestricted for parents, 8 A.M. to 8 P.M. for others. Telephones are available for the children to call home, and parents are encouraged to leave dimes for the children for this purpose. A hospital mailing address is given so a child can receive mail. A descriptive list of the workers whom the parent may meet identifies various members of the hospital staff. There is a description of what the child's behavior may be after he comes home from the hospital, with some clues to the parent on how to deal with it. The suggestion is made that if the child's reaction to hospitalization seems excessive or lasts a long time, the parent may wish to speak to the doctor about it.

In the old building there were single rooms in which mothers could live in with their children on 3 of the 6 divisions; on other divisions arrangements were frequently made for mothers to stay in the multiple-bed rooms. In the new building every division has its own single-room facilities, with the exception of the premature babies' nursery. As the premature babies become stronger, however, they are transferred to a division in which the mother can live in before the baby is discharged.

With premature babies, as well as with every other child admitted, the mothers are encouraged and taught to participate in care. In many cases this means learning to handle equipment and follow special procedures. This policy indicates the emphasis on communication and cooperation between staff and parents.

Children of like ages were put together on all divisions in the old building, except in the surgical division, which had children of all ages. In the new hospital there are 2 surgical divisions, which makes it possible to group the children by age there.

Despite the sophisticated equipment and care in this hospital, the atmosphere is casual and nonthreatening. The division for toddlers, for instance, has, in addition to the playroom, a play space at one end. The children wander from the toys and television set to their cribs, using the entire area for play. Several comfortable chairs are available for mothers, and although they may talk with and read to children other than their own, they can give care only to their own child. Toy bags are tied to the beds, and the children wear their own clothes whenever possible. The hospital provides play clothes for those children who have not brought their own clothing.

On a typical morning, one mother is patiently restraining

her 2-year-old from taking off a mist mask until the allotted time is up while exchanging casual remarks with the nurse, who neither interferes with the mother's handling of the child nor addresses herself to the child directly. She has stopped for a moment to supervise the procedure and to help if necessary, but she has left the entire authority with the mother and the effect is very much as if two mothers had stopped for a moment to chat in a park or playground, neither asserting any jurisdiction over the other.

Another nurse on the same division is followed by an insistent 3-year-old boy. She has suggested various occupations in the play area, but he has refused them all and still clings closely to her. She puts a hand on his head with casual affection and says with a little laugh, "Well, I guess you are going to have to come along then and help me with my work!" He follows her quite happily around the area and out into the hall, much in the way that he might have followed his mother doing housework at home.

This friendly acceptance of parents and the warm informality on the part of the nurses that seem to pervade so much of the hospital were not always the rule at Babies and Childrens Hospital. How did this attitude come about and why does it seem so successful with both nursing staff and parents?

It is very difficult to pinpoint the exact date of the hospital nursing staff's increasing awareness of the importance of "family-centered care." It grew gradually and was a result of a group effort to provide quality child care that would involve the parents. In the early 1960's the nursing leadership group began concentrating more emphasis on psychological aspects of child care, which led to the establishment of unlimited visiting hours. These new hours resulted in an increasing number of parents visiting and staying with their children over longer periods of time. The nurses became aware that it was necessary to spend more time with parents in order to support them in their parental role and provide them with an opportunity to participate in the care of their children. Intensive staff development conferences were initiated to assist the nurses in particular, and other personnel to a lesser extent, in understanding the role of the mother in the hospital and how the functions of the nurse, licensed practical nurse, and nursing aide would have to change. These conferences were most helpful in implementing and evaluating the program. Now, in the 1970's, family-centered care is an accepted and functional philosophy, and this climate permeates all levels of the nursing staff and to a very great extent is operational in other disciplines such as medicine, dietary services, social services, and others. Working in close partnership with parents is not easy, but the staff and administration feel it is the best and most meaningful way to provide quality care to the child and support to the parents.

The director of pediatric nursing at Babies and Childrens Hospital confirms the need for sustained effort on the part of those interested in making changes. An important step in inaugurating new points of view, she feels, is that of letting staff members participate in the discussions concerning change and encouraging them to express worries and feelings that may arise in connection with innovations. It is normal to resist change while ideas are new and theories untried.

As parents took more part in their children's care, most of the nurses found the new atmosphere very rewarding. The general feeling now is that when parents are with their children the children not only receive greater emotional support, but the quality of care given by the nurses is actually improved by the parent's presence. This is possible because the close parent-nurse communication enables the nurse to gain insight into many needs of the child which might otherwise not be apparent. Although there is occasionally a problem one, parents can be of great help to the nurse because of their special expertise with their own children; this is often seen in their handling of hospital procedures as well as in their management of feeding, toileting, and many other daily activities. The hospital believes there is less crying on the divisions when parents are present and that children adapt to treatments such as anesthesia better when the parents are allowed to be in the hospital with them.

The director of pediatric nursing states, "Our policy is well established, and we screen for nurses who have an interest in working with parents." She has reorganized the hospital nursing staff aimed at freeing nurses for their primary activities of bedside care and close involvement with children and families. By relieving them of hospital administration duties and paper work through the use of division coordinators and secretaries, she hopes to gain more and improved child care and teaching of parents.

Pediatric nurses are highly skilled and very valuable. There seems never to be enough supply for the demand. Therefore, they should be free to do the work for which they were prepared—the practice of nursing. The leadership personnel in pediatric nursing are in a position to observe and facilitate what they term "reeducating nurses" to their role and freeing them to carry it out.

Hardly anything can happen in the hospital without affecting other departments. Any change affects everyone— all the disciplines have an effect on the care of the child—so we have to understand what we are doing and each discipline has to understand what the other is doing. Interdisciplinary communication is vital.

One important goal of continuing education in pediatrics should be to teach young nurses and house officers to take the family into account and to learn how to relate to the child in his family context. Much of the care of children must include parents. Nurses and physicians who come from settings that did not provide them much background in this concept see parents on the divisions here, become acquainted with them, and learn to implement this point of view more fully.

When the divisions are observed to see what this philosophy of relating to parents consists of in day-to-day contacts, certain departures from traditional hospital practice are very visible: A mother is bathing her child and the child is laughing and enjoying herself as she would be at home. A father is allowed to go into the humidity room to reassure his child who is apprehensive about the unfamiliar atmosphere. An ambulatory little girl, dressed for out-of-doors, is going down the hall with a young nurse. The senior clinical nurse stops to speak with them. It appears that the little girl had no visitors yesterday and will have none today, so she and the nurse are going on a short expedition to look at the world outside and then to the cafeteria to have a soft drink, "just for a change."

A night supervisor talks of new patients in a way that makes one realize that the concept of supporting the hospitalized child emotionally has permeated the entire 24-hour nursing staff.

We don't like to rush the parents or the child. After all, the situation is difficult and sometimes frightening to them. We let the child stay in his own clothes and take a little time to relax and look around and get settled. We find that if the child and his mother are reassured, it is easier for them and the nurses to handle the nursing care requirements, and routines go more smoothly. We attempt to get across to the mother and/or father that they are welcome to stay and let them know that we think their child will be better off if they do.

This same night supervisor also indicated that the nurses at Babies and Childrens Hospital show perception about those parents who are under too much stress, ill at ease, or perhaps rejecting their children. This is particularly true of parents who have been staying with their critically ill children continuously, or with the parent of a child who is in surgery. Sometimes a nurse who has time or is leaving for the day will invite a mother apparently under stress to have coffee with her on the division or in the hospital coffee shop as relaxation. One senior clinical nurse described how she attempts to assist mothers who appear to be ill at ease about staying and those who appear to be rejecting. She starts by explaining to the mother the child's feelings of uncertainty and fear about separation, the need for him to know if the mother is coming back, and his anxieties about being with strange people in a strange situation in which he might be hurt. She suggests that the mother visit and tell the child honestly when she has to leave and when she will be back. After a while, if things go well, the nurse can ask the mother if she would like to feed the child at mealtime, a situation with which the child and mother are both familiar and in which they are usually at ease. This nurse stresses, "But you can't push. You have to let parents move one step at a time, and you should be cognizant of and responsive to their feelings and anxieties as well as to those of the child." If parents don't visit at all, or visit seldom and seem out of touch with the hospital, the nurses call in a pediatric social worker. The social worker, in turn, attempts to contact the parents directly or will make contact with the appropriate community agency. Often it is only a matter of the social worker assisting the mother to make better plans about visiting. In this hospital nurses may make direct referrals of such cases to the Department of Social Service, after which either the nurse or the social worker communicates to the doctor that this has been done.

Both Babies and Childrens Hospital and Children's Hospital of Philadelphia dramatically illustrate that older facilities need not be an insuperable obstacle to personalized and sympathetic care.

REFERENCES

Barnett, C., Leiderman, P. H., and Grobstein, R. Neonatal separation: The maternal side of interactional deprivation. *Pediatrics* 45:197-205, 1970.

Bear, E. Operation open heart. *Nursing Outlook* 10:158-161, 1962.

Blake, F. G. *The Child, His Parents and the Nurse.* Philadelphia: Lippincott, 1954.

Blumgart, E., and Korsch, B. Pediatric recreation: An approach to meeting the needs of hospitalized children. *Pediatrics* 34:133-136, 1964.

Brooks, M. M. Play for hospitalized children. *Young Children* 24:219-224, 1969.

Brooks, M. M. How ya gonna keep them down? *New York Times Magazine,* April 5, 1970. Pp. 97-109.

Heavenrich, R. Viewpoints on children in hospitals. *Hospitals* 37:40-46, 1963.

Jessner, L., Blom, G., and Waldfogel, S. Emotional implications of tonsillectomy and adenoidectomy on children. *Psychoanalytic Study of the Child* 7:126-169, 1952.

Lipton, S. On the psychology of childhood tonsillectomy. *Psychoanalytic Study of the Child* 17:363-417, 1962.

MacKeith, R. Children in hospital, preparation for operation. *Lancet* 2:843, 1953.

Mahaffy, P. R. The effects of hospitalization on children admitted for tonsillectomy and adenoidectomy. *Nursing Research* 14:12-20, 1965.

Mellish, R. W. P. Preparation of the child for hospitalization and surgery. *Pediatric Clinics of North America* 16:543-553, 1969.

5

Advocates and Ombudsmen

CHANGES in hospital policy can often be traced to a few dedicated persons, the most obvious change agents being members of the medical staff, whose influence in any hospital is strong and far-reaching. Dr. Henry Kempe and Dr. Henry Silver at the University of Colorado Medical Center and Dr. Robert E. Cooke at The Johns Hopkins Hospital Children's Medical and Surgical Center have created an atmosphere and a physical setting for parent involvement. Sometimes medicine and nursing together implement new policies: Dr. Joseph H. Patterson and Miss Margaret Bodeker set guidelines and policies for the Henrietta Egleston Hospital and influenced the building design so parent participation would be facilitated.

Dr. Joseph Butterfield at The Children's Hospital, Denver, planned and implemented the policy of a Newborn Center in a hospital which has an otherwise conservative attitude toward families; the attitude of the Newborn Center toward parents is markedly different from that of the rest of the hospital. Here Dr. Butterfield was, and is, the prime mover for change, getting the space for the unit by converting what was an intensive care unit, setting guidelines for staff, and carrying out innovative details.

Similarly, Dr. T. Berry Brazelton at the Children's Hospital Medical Center of Boston has initiated some policy changes, especially in a long-term care unit, the House of the Good Samaritan. However, his commitment to total care is only partially reflected in the policies of the hospital in general.

Sometimes change takes place in a hospital with the creation of a single new position that fills a previously unrecognized need and crosses lines traditionally drawn between departments. Such a position may bring about change by the mere fact that it exists and will often facilitate new kinds of communication among departments. New positions can be initiated in various ways: of the eight persons whose jobs are discussed in this chapter, four are employed by the pediatric department, three are directly employed by the department of nursing, and one is directly responsible to the Department of Child Psychiatry. All have a certain flexibility of jurisdiction in that they are not confined to limited areas. Although some are involved in carrying out play or recreational activities, their scope is not limited only to these programs.

CLEVELAND METROPOLITAN GENERAL HOSPITAL

In the early 1950's Anna Freud lectured in Cleveland on the needs of hospitalized children. The many professionals who heard her were impressed with the necessity for meeting those needs in the hospitals of which they were a part. Among them was Dr. Frederick Robbins, then director of pediatrics at Cleveland Metropolitan General Hospital, a teaching hospital of Case Western Reserve University. He arranged for Mrs. Emma Plank, a specialist in early childhood development who was to become one of the best-known pioneers in the ombudsman role, to join the staff as director of the Child Life and Education Program. Mrs. Plank has been with the hospital since 1955, and her program and influence reach into all sections of pediatric care and extend beyond the hospital into university teaching. She is consultant for another Cleveland hospital and lectures to community groups. Her book *Working with Children in Hospitals*[1] has become a classic in its field. As director of the Child Life and Education Program, Mrs. Plank carries out a complex job on many levels and supervises her staff as well as students in training. She and two medical students have undertaken a study of children on their first admission to pediatrics to ascertain the emotional impact of their first experiences with the strange hospital world. But of major significance here is the way in which she sees the needs of the child and the role of her staff and herself in relationship to him. Primarily, Mrs. Plank sees each child in a personal and individual way. To understand this very personal awareness of each child, one should look first at the setting in which Mrs. Plank's department carries out its program.

Cleveland Metropolitan General Hospital is a large, 143-year-old county hospital that serves the urban and county population of Cleveland and has grown somewhat shabby and overcrowded along the way. Remodeling continues to give more badly needed space. Once the center for communicable diseases and the only hospital for the indigent population, it

---

[1]Plank, E. *Working with Children in Hospitals.* Cleveland, Ohio: Case Western Reserve University Press, 1962.

now serves more and more as the primary medical facility for families in a fifteen-block radius in its own neighborhood.

The hospital deals primarily with two populations: the stable urban black group and the more migratory and newer influx of people from Appalachia. The Appalachian population, transitory, paternally oriented, and somewhat clannish and self-contained, is harder to reach than the urban group. The staff expresses concern that too many of these families have failed to avail themselves of the hospital's facilities. The hospital uses social casework and interacts with outside agencies for contact with and follow-up of the families. Homemaker services and transportation funds are made available, and in special situations parents may stay overnight at the nurses' residence near the hospital.

When a child is admitted, he and his parents are given a booklet illustrated with appealing photographs of children in the wards unpacking, eating, playing, and in cribs. The text stresses the parents' role with the child. It is simply written, two or three paragraphs to a page, with an opening statement that is supportive for parent and child: "Both you and your child may feel a lot better about coming to the hospital if you know what to expect. This little book tells the story. It will help you to explain to him some of the frightening aspects of a hospital stay to reassure him."

Below is a space to enter the name of the child's doctor and the section and division of the hospital in which the child will stay. The booklet indicates that the parent may visit the child at meals and feed him, join him in the inpatient playroom and the outdoor play area, and visit him in isolation. The section on visiting rules reads in part: "You, the parents, are the most important people to your child. Therefore, come regularly to visit . . . Tell the nurse in charge when you plan to visit again so she can comfort your child if he should become sad waiting for you. Don't get upset if he cries when you leave. This is quite natural but be sure to tell him when you will be back and when his daddy can come too."

The booklet covers many other subjects. On surgery, the parent is told to make every effort to be with the child: "Be sure to be at his bedside when he returns to the ward." There are suggestions on the kinds of toys to bring, and a mailing address for the child is given with a suggestion that he be sent cards and letters. On the final page the parent is told what to expect when the child goes home after hospitalization, with the emphasis on reassuring the parents about the child's behavior and clues on how to help him.

Each division has a parent waiting room. Patients anxious about home may have visits from their siblings in the outdoor playground or in an office.

Parents take no active part in the care of their premature babies. They may visit their children in the intensive care unit within limitations, although only on rare occasions are parents actively involved with their children in this unit.

The Child Life and Education staff concentrates on the patient himself while the social service department takes responsibility for dealing with the parent, the home situation, and the community factors outside the hospital. Nurses handle parent counseling related to the child's care; in so doing they help the mothers carry out some procedures for their children and make special arrangements on the rare occasions when the mothers spend the night. They also discuss the child's progress with the mother and consult with the Child Life and Education staff on family needs and on how best to win the mother's confidence.

The Child Life and Education staff helps prepare the child for surgery. They read and discuss with the child a book which outlines the steps of surgery; they invite the child's questions to clarify misunderstandings and to deal with his fears. A member of the staff often accompanies a child to surgery, particularly if the parent cannot be there, explains the procedures to him ahead of time, and allows him to express his feelings afterward. Sometimes the staff is better able to prepare the child for surgery than a mother, who may, because of her own situation, become anxious, upset, or even angry. Children often respond well to a person who is calm and not unduly anxious about the outcome and who is not emotionally involved.

Cleveland Metropolitan General Hospital seems not to differ from many traditional hospitals: the wards often are crowded, little space is available for play tables and children's activities, beds and cribs tend to be close together, the distances between wards can be long, and the halls are busy. But in the presence of Mrs. Plank and her staff lies the significant difference. Of primary importance is their equality with the medical and nursing staffs and the administration, which gives Mrs. Plank the authority to implement policies and to consult with the heads of departments.

On one typical day, while she goes on rounds, her office is used by a member of her staff for special counseling with a 6-year-old boy who is in the hospital for surgery and is emotionally upset as well. The office becomes a quiet refuge for him and his particular friend on the staff, who is acting as therapist, mother surrogate, and tutor.

Mrs. Plank goes to the toddlers' ward, greeting staff and children. A 2-year-old standing in bed is looking sorrowfully at a breakfast tray on a table nearby. In a brief conference with the nurse, Mrs. Plank finds that the child is not allowed breakfast because he is scheduled for tests, so she suggests to the nurse that the tray be taken away so that he will not be tantalized. She spends some time explaining to the child just why there will be no breakfast, tells him that his doctor will be coming soon, and promises that he will have things to eat later on. She leaves him smiling as she waves to him from the door.

She stops in the hall to greet a child who is being wheeled to a playroom, stops again to talk to a child in an iron lung, and starts down the long halls and up the elevators to other wards. On the way, at one of the research units, she picks up a 7-year-old boy. He must be back in the unit later for a test but is bored now, so he is invited to accompany her and proudly goes ahead down the halls, ringing for elevators and occasionally dropping back to talk.

Upstairs, a large ward is almost empty; the children being either in treatment or in the playrooms. Mrs. Plank confers with the nursing staff and checks on the activities of particular children. She stops in the playroom where the children and an aide are busy with film strips to introduce the little boy to the group and to make sure that he will be accompanied back to his unit in time for his tests.

Then there is a short visit to the infant nursery where a young father in a rocking chair holds his baby girl. A nurse sits near, enjoying the domesticity of father and child but not interfering. There is general admiration of the baby and congratulations to the father before Mrs. Plank goes on her way.

The outdoor playground is down more long halls and down a steep flight of stairs. Here she sits down by the sandbox to talk to a mother visiting her child. She admires the child's accomplishments and talks with the mother about making haste slowly.

"One of the things we must guard against," says Mrs. Plank, "is pushing a child beyond his capabilities when we begin to see progress. A long-term patient here may spend a weekend at home and come back overly tired because the parents have been so pleased with his abilities that they have allowed him to do too much. We have to support and educate the parents in letting him progress at his own capacity."

After contacts with three other children supervised by a nurse, it is time to meet with two social workers for lunch in the hospital cafeteria. Then she must leave for a speaking engagement in another city.

Often she makes these rounds to wards, playrooms, and playground several times a day, visiting with many different departments and holding conversations with many people. During this long trip around the hospital the focus has been on the children's needs.

First, a child has been given special help and personal understanding in the office by a member of the staff, who has concentrated on him away from the larger and more confusing hospital world. The many children whom Mrs. Plank visited were made aware that someone understood how they were feeling: a breakfast tray tantalizing a little boy who wasn't allowed breakfast, a boring morning in an adult-oriented unit suddenly changed to an expedition that ended in a film show, the monotony of being immobilized in an iron lung being understood by someone who cared and new interests being planned. These are ways of showing a child that, even though the parents may not be there, someone is in a parental position and sees the child as an individual.

"In a large hospital like this with many people around and with teaching rounds," says Mrs. Plank, "a child may be at the mercy of a constant series of surface contacts with strangers. Shallow, brief, and casual contacts all day long can add to a child's confusion and perhaps intensify an emotional upset, without serving any valid purpose." For this reason,

Cleveland Metropolitan General Hospital does not use volunteers or Foster Grandparents, and there is only one occupational therapist. Mrs. Plank and her staff try to keep up consistent relationships with the children, based on each child's particular needs, and they work to avoid meaningless social clichés and smiles to which a child may feel obliged to respond.

During her rounds, Mrs. Plank took the opportunity to talk to nurses about particular children, to make suggestions, and to encourage those nurses who had questions or problems. She reinforced a father's pride and closeness to his baby, and she encouraged the mother on the playground about her child's progress. One of the main tenets of her policy is giving parents a feeling of success. "We want them to know that they are doing a good job and contributing to the child's getting well. If we can do it by freeing them to do a job at home, or by having them here, or by showing them how to help with a procedure—it's all part of the same thing. We want them to know that they are good parents and doing something well."

Some mothers, often educationally deprived, of very low income, or who do not speak English, may need special support. The best help for such families may be to reaffirm the mother's role at home and to supplement the child's experience in the hospital with parent surrogates. In many cases the parents might not be able to tolerate long visiting with the child or rooming in, while the family at home would find it difficult to accept the absence of the mother. Giving the parent "permission" to be at home, and at the same time helping the child to face the hospital situation without losing contact with his home, is often more realistic than just seeing that a parent stays with the child, particularly when the family lives in an area nearby.

Mrs. Plank's chief concern is with the experience of the

child in the hospital, but public health nurses and social workers are valuable in helping the family at home.

One typical example of this interdisciplinary cooperation is the case of a 14-year-old girl who was admitted to the hospital for a spinal fusion. Partly because her relationship with her mother was difficult, she had left home the year before coming to the hospital and had lived alone in Chicago. She was immobilized in the hospital for a long time, and when her mother visited her the situation was not easy for either. The Child Life and Education staff focused its efforts on dealing directly with the girl, who seemed relieved to talk to friends who were not part of her complicated home situation. A consulting psychiatrist was called in to interview the girl and to help both the girl and the department in dealing with the family. Medical social workers in the hospital also took on the problems of the home, to plan ahead for the situation that would face the child when she was discharged from the hospital.

Mrs. Plank or a member of her staff will sometimes spend several hours a day with a child such as this or one who seems to have a particular problem. They consider the one-to-one relationship not only a help to the child, but a way of avoiding the spread of emotional upset to the other children, since a disturbed child may well become a disruptive force.

The Child Life and Education staff are flexible in the methods they use. An older child on a ward will sometimes be enlisted to help a younger one; a "foster-sibling" relationship between two hospitalized children can sometimes be very rewarding for both, providing a homelike give-and-take, with "mothering" for the younger child and satisfaction and achievement for the older one. Visits with siblings from home are often arranged.

A liaison role between the child and the many influences

on him, and the authority of her status, make it possible for Mrs. Plank to coordinate services and situations in the child's best interest and at the same time to relieve the nursing and medical staff of many demands. With professionals and with outside groups she works in the same way to facilitate understanding and thus ease the difficulties for parent, professional, and child during hospitalization. In addition, she goes into the community to talk to college classes or to parents' groups on the emotional needs of sick children, about preparing children for the hospital, and about the ways hospitalization can enhance growth.

THE MOUNT SINAI HOSPITAL OF CLEVELAND

A role similar to Mrs. Plank's, but in quite a different kind of setting, is held by Mrs. Anna Bond, social group worker in pediatrics at The Mount Sinai Hospital of Cleveland, a nonprofit community hospital housed in an attractive modern building. The pediatric division has pleasant colors and the walls are hung with pictures by children. Cots are available by a child's bed for parents. In order to encourage parent visiting, the social work department provides vouchers for taxi transportation and offers homemaker services in cases of individual need.

The policy of the pediatric division is one of encouraging the continuing physical presence of the parent during critical situations—for instance, before and after surgery parents are helped to see the need for honest preparation of the child. The child who knows that his mother is being truthful about when she can visit, who is not deceived about what is going on, and who trusts the staff of the hospital will have more positive feelings and be less apt to need a parent with him all the time, Mrs. Bond tells parents and staff.

Brothers and sisters may visit at Mount Sinai. It is especially important that a twin be allowed to visit, says Mrs. Bond, since twins are interdependent. Visits are arranged with the child's special needs in mind.

At a parents' meeting, one mother who was discussing the situation at home said, "My husband asks and asks—he just drives me crazy wanting to know everything the doctor said and every little thing that goes on. He pesters me about it all the time." This led to a discussion of whether fathers felt left out when mothers spent large amounts of time with a hospitalized child, and whether the father might like to talk to the doctor or come to see the nurses and pediatric unit for himself. The mother, until that time, had not considered that the father might ask his questions of anyone but herself, and she was thinking over the idea as the meeting ended.

The parents' meetings are conducted weekly by Mrs. Bond and are attended also by at least one member of the nursing staff, the social case worker, and one or more of the students from Case Western Reserve University interning in social group work under the supervision of Mrs. Bond. They are scheduled for one o'clock in the afternoon, in the waiting room down a hallway from the pediatric division. The room has comfortable chairs and low tables with ashtrays and magazines. Always open to parents, it is usually occupied by several, sometimes accompanied by their children, reading the available pamphlets on child development and care or talking with each other. The hospital supplies coffee and cookies for the weekly meetings, and a nurse or social worker invites the parents informally in advance.

"Parents share information," says Mrs. Bond, "and this sharing can have destructive aspects, resulting in misunderstanding of what is happening or of the child's needs, as well as accidentally passing along misinformation. Our meetings help direct parents to the appropriate sources of information, and we can also interpret such realities as why a doctor may not be available when a parent wishes to see him. We try to encourage active participation. Parents need to ask "what" and "why." We as staff reassure them that we do not discuss anything that has been said in confidence, and we try to encourage them to be sensitive to each other's feelings."

Parents are told of the meetings when the child is admitted, and there are further informal invitations just before a meeting starts. Mothers sometimes attend with a child, who is welcomed, and the discussions include explanations by various staff members of their roles and ways in which they can help parents, and of standard procedures and routines such as family-style meals and bedtime. Mothers bring up any topics they consider important and often reassure and support each other. The tone is social and casual; in one such group the mothers discussed in detail the difficulty of explaining to a child that the parents were not able to take him home. Mrs. Bond and her staff assured the concerned parents that a group worker would help the child understand that going home was at the discretion of the doctor and not an arbitrary decision on the part of the parents. At that same meeting, a case worker explained her role, emphasizing that she was available to help with home problems and finances at the request of any parents. "I don't try to tell parents what they should do, and I don't press them if they say they don't want me, but if there is a problem I let them know that there are all kinds of solutions."

Bimonthly staff meetings include the director and assistant director of pediatrics, the chief pediatric resident, pediatric case workers, nursing instructor, head nurses, occupational therapist, group worker, and psychiatrist. The child's relationship with his family and the special needs of the family are a part of the discussions. Case presentations three times a month include the case workers and the pediatric group worker. At these conferences the group worker presents a picture of the child-family behavior as observed in the hospital. The case worker may help the family directly or may be the agent through which the particular problem of the family is referred to an outside agency.

The Child Life and Education Program facilitates informal communication among all services on the floor, and planning is shared. This is not an attempt to blur the distinction between areas of responsibility; on the contrary, it leads to greater respect for particular areas of expertise. Students are allowed to read the nurses' notes, and this sharing of information has improved the quality of the nurses' records: notes have become more informative and less routine than they were in the past.

Nurses who find a particular parent difficult—for instance, a mother who is hostile about the way she thinks her child is being treated—are encouraged to talk about their feelings with the social worker in appropriate groups. They may discuss the home situation, the mother's reaction, and what the care plan has been. In failure-to-thrive cases in which a neglected child improves noticeably during his stay in the hospital, a nurse's feelings about releasing the child to the parents may be difficult to handle. The case worker and the social group worker can be useful both in helping make the family situation better for the child and in helping the nursing staff handle its own feelings toward the family.

Mrs. Bond discusses the different areas of responsibility and interdisciplinary communication.

We never do each other's job. We depend on and respect each other's job. This is a hospital, after all. The nursing staff is responsible for the floor. Any changes must be channeled through the authority of the nurses in charge. When we are most helpful is in taking on the nonmedical problems that make for difficult situations. For instance, a 5-year-old boy who was hospitalized for intestinal obstruction was upset and worried. The nurse found out and told us that he believed he was pregnant. Here was a case in which we could help the nurse by talking to the child and allowing him to express his ideas and his fears and by giving him clear answers and reassurance. I am here most of the time; we can see when a mother is anxious or when she is hampering the nurses' job; we can see how children are reacting.

Communication between parents and staff, between children and staff, between professionals in the different disciplines, and between parent and parent for mutual support through a difficult experience is the keynote of The Mount Sinai Hospital of Cleveland's social group workers' program.

BOSTON FLOATING HOSPITAL FOR INFANTS AND CHILDREN

Acting as ombudsman in Boston Floating Hospital, Mrs. Kristine Angoff moves through all the units, supplying appropriate bedside toys and making personal contact with the patients; the "toy rounds" may sometimes be delegated to one of the staff of four full-time nursery school teachers. She also supervises the playroom and the activities of the student teacher assistants who augment her regular staff.

Boston Floating Hospital centers much of its nonmedical concern for children around the top-floor playroom. Each morning one of the play staff visits children confined to bed, bringing them age-suitable toys and discussing their interests and progress; another staff member consults the head nurse of each ward to learn which children may make use of the playroom and notes the medical restrictions on the activity of each.

The medical staff and administration of the hospital are a constant support, both financially and in making referrals, to the playroom program (in operation since 1947 as part of the Child Psychiatry Unit). As many ambulatory children as possible spend at least part of the day there. Through the hospital psychiatrists, the staff of the play program has an unusual opportunity to help children with individual problems and often to help parents understand and find new ways of reacting to difficult situations.

Several facets of this play program are unusual. Since it is part of the Child Psychiatry Unit, emphasis is on understanding the total child in the context of his background and family. The playroom has a one-way mirror and microphone so that a psychiatrist or other professional may observe the children's behavior. The frequent consultations between play staff and psychiatrists, augmented by observations made by the nurses on the wards and observations in the playroom, can give a very clear picture of a child's emotional and developmental needs. A second unusual aspect of the program is the structuring of the relationship between the children and the play staff. A research study program carried out on the play patterns of hospitalized children from 3 to 10 years old showed unmistakably that while children of grade-school age were able to find support and comfort with companions of their own age, children 3 and 4 years old need the active approach of an adult to help them overcome their grief and sense of abandonment. Without this adult help they became listless, aimless, and unable to mobilize their energies. The play program is thus structured so that each teacher has in her special care a small group of children to whom she becomes a mother substitute. These groups include children of various ages: the younger ones can find security in physical contact with a mothering person who will hold them, give them a lap to sit on, and supply toys and encouragement. Children 4 and 5 years old find their newly emerging independence shaken, so they may regress temporarily to a previous, more dependent level of development. These children are reassured and encouraged when they are able to put their trust in a teacher who is with them for many hours and shows her personal concern and interest in them. Once this trust is established, they are often able to work through their fears and feelings by using the playroom to act out their experiences in play, thus gaining mastery of them.

The playroom, with its "families" of children centered about each teacher, is open from 9:30 A.M. to 12 P.M. and from 2 P.M. to 4 P.M. Midday meals are often served there from a small kitchen (part of the unit), which also holds snacks and fruit juices for playtime breaks. On occasion, nurses have given simple medications and carried out dressing changes in the playroom with the permission of the medical staff, rather than fragmenting the child's day and depriving him of the ongoing presence of an adult to whom he looks for reassurance.

Parents may join the children here during the afternoon hours, and their visits often have a dimension beyond that of simply being with the child in a pleasant atmosphere. Mrs. Angoff and her teaching staff take advantage of the parents' presence to answer questions and sometimes to give them a place of refuge with their children from the more public wards. The mother of a child who is mentally retarded as well as ill, for instance, may feel self-conscious about how other visiting parents view him. A particular illness or condition may make the parents feel that the child is conspicuous, which makes them anxious to protect the child. In the playroom with its sympathetic staff and acceptant and sheltering atmosphere, the parents are more easily able to relax and enjoy being with their children. Often, too, they can observe their child's interaction with others and gain new understanding of his behavior.

This opportunity to be with the children is not the only use that adults make of the playroom. After play hours are over, staff members may meet individual parents here to talk about the child or about the parent's own problems, or to familiarize them with the kinds of play and the materials that the children are offered. Sometimes parents come here simply for respite, an interval of calm from the tension and uncertainty of being with a child on the wards. Occasionally parents have used the playroom and the sympathetic interest of its staff as an opportunity for emotional outbursts, a relief from the restraint they have exercised when they are with their children. The playroom thus has multiple uses: as a laboratory for studying the needs of the children, as a homelike situation in which trust and confidence can be fostered between the child and a caring adult, and as a place of refuge for parents and children who are under special stress.

The play program has, in addition, a particularly important role in the hospital: the teachers carry out long-term therapeutic plans with selected patients under the supervision of the Child Psychiatry Unit. These patients, whose stay in the hospital will be longer than average, usually fall into two categories: failure-to-thrive children in whom there is no serious organic defect and in whom emotional deprivation seems to be the cause of the condition; and children who have a severe emotional reaction to a serious illness with prolonged hospitalization. Plans for these particular children are structured and carried out by teamwork between the psychiatrist and the play teacher and depend on a continuity of relationship between the child and an adult, with emphasis on careful planning and psychiatric supervision.

To augment the playroom itself and the toy rounds, which begin at 8:30 every morning, there are areas on the wards that have tables for play and for family-style meals. (The playroom staff also supplies the outpatient clinic waiting rooms with toys, which the children use under the supervision of their parents since no staff is on duty there.) The general atmosphere of all the play areas is informal and permissive, and toys are readily available.

The play areas incorporated into the wards themselves help many of the hospital's short-term patients find satisfying activities and the company of playmates close at hand. The playroom, with its more specialized function of personalized care, is thus made available to the children who need it most.

Interaction with the psychiatric staff and the remarkably varied programs are useful to many kinds of patients, some immobilized in bed and some ambulatory, many with emotional as well as physical problems. Parents as well as children are the concern of the staff. The playroom's research, function, and influence on professional staff led to the design of the Family Participation Unit, discussed in Chapter 2. One element in its success is undoubtedly the support and backing it receives from the Child Psychiatry Unit and the exchange of information and insights with it.

Another element is surely the dedication of Mrs. Angoff, who, like Mrs. Plank at Cleveland Metropolitan General Hospital, considers all the children her responsibility and acts on their behalf on many levels.

NEW YORK HOSPITAL-CORNELL MEDICAL CENTER

Miss Madeline Petrillo, M.Ed., the mental health consultant to the pediatric nursing staff at New York Hospital-Cornell Medical Center in New York City, has a liaison position between nursing staff, patient, and medical staff which makes it possible for her to bridge some of the gaps in understanding that often arise in a large, multidisciplinary institution. Her services are available to the nurses and medical staff of any pediatric unit who need help with the care of children presenting behavior problems while hospitalized.

During the five years she has been with the hospital, Miss Petrillo has developed a program through which staff members have become increasingly aware of the needs of children of various ages and through which they are able to develop skills for communicating with, and working with, children and their families. Besides conducting classes for nurses, she counsels individually with young patients and sometimes with their parents. Like the other ombudsmen mentioned previously, who see their role as a flexible one serving all of pediatrics, she makes visits to many units, sometimes bringing play materials that will help a child and sometimes coming for conferences with staff members.

One successful technique Miss Petrillo has developed for the nursing staff is the use of replicas of hospital equipment.

A doll in an oxygen tent, a miniature intravenous setup, actual medicine droppers, and syringes with a real needle are manipulated by the child to give him a feeling of mastery over the procedures and an understanding of what will happen. She also uses simple outlines on which the organs of the body can be drawn to explain anatomy and physiology. "Patient" dolls, which are made to her specifications oy hospital volunteers and dressed in hospital clothing, are often used to familiarize a child with bandages, dressings, tubes, and other medical appliances. Even quite young children are helped, with these dolls, to visualize what they themselves will look like after surgery—with bandages or in an inhalation tent.

Miss Petrillo very much prefers to include parents in the preparation of a child for surgery, partly to encourage them in a feeling of participation in their child's care and partly to reinforce the positive feelings of the child. She finds that many parents who have had doubts about their own abilities to explain the situation to the child are relieved to share this responsibility and are very helpful. When parents are reluctant to take part, or reluctant to have the child informed about forthcoming procedures for fear of frightening him, Miss Petrillo and the nursing staff try to concentrate first on the needs of the parents and then on helping them understand what will ease the situation for the child.

As at Children's Hospital of Philadelphia, the nursing department of New York Hospital-Cornell Medical Center took the initiative when they saw the need for a position such as Miss Petrillo's. She was engaged by the director of the Department of Pediatric Nursing with the full support of the director of nursing, who is also the dean of the School of Nursing.

The way in which her position and influence have grown

since she has been with the hospital is enlightening, particularly when seen in relation to the many hospitals in the country that seem unable to implement any closer and more understanding relationship with children and their parents because of administrative or departmental slowdowns or lack of interest. Hired primarily to facilitate understanding of behavior problems in hospitalized children, Miss Petrillo found initially that she was without a clearly defined role and without status. Her initial premise—that much regressive behavior and many disciplinary problems could be modified by the ways in which they were handled by the staff—gave rise to some skepticism and natural defensiveness on the part of those professionals already burdened with large caseloads. Miss Petrillo was sure that a program to help with emotional and behavioral problems in children would mean more cooperative patients and more job satisfaction for the staff.

She made her services available to any nurse on any unit who needed assistance. Requests were slow in coming, and indeed, the first requests were in the form of turning over to her completely, and sometimes with a sigh of relief, patients who were thought to be unusually difficult and uncooperative. Instead of being used as a consultant, she found herself to be a special resource for dealing with what were considered to be insoluble patient problems. "On the principle that one begins at the level of readiness," she says cheerfully, "this was where the program started—at a point at which there was little disagreement among the nurses on how they could benefit, and at which they agreed that there were patients whose needs were not being met."

She started working with a withdrawn and regressive 4-year-old who had been in isolation for over a month because of extensive burns. As her communication with the child improved, Miss Petrillo kept the nursing staff informed of the basic concepts she was using and about the progress of the child, who was then beginning to react well to the nurses. For about a month she continued working with the child and demonstrating progress to the staff, who began to put into operation some of her techniques for reversing the child's regression. This pragmatic and direct use of her skills, and the educational value of having them demonstrated, led to her initiation of a course for the staff in child growth and development and the management of typical behavior problems. Staff interest increased, and a second case of difficult behavior on which she and a nurse worked together led to such dramatic improvement on the child's part that he became the subject of a nursing team conference. This, in turn, led to a series of conferences on related subjects, and from it emerged a general plan for preparing children for urological surgery. Eventually this plan of preparation was modified for use in other situations, and a similar plan is now being used to prepare all surgical patients and patients undergoing diagnostic testing.

After a year it was possible to see increasing acceptance of and participation in Miss Petrillo's program by the nursing staff. Today, all the pediatric units are involved in both the preparation of children for surgery and in the handling of emotional and behavioral problems. Some particular situations present areas of difficulty because of the size and arrangement of the hospital. For instance, patients scheduled for tonsillectomy and other surgical patients are often housed in a surgical ward intended primarily for adults and therefore not easily accessible to pediatric nurses. However, after Miss Petrillo's assistant made regular visits to the children there as part of the pediatric program, the surgical department appointed a full-time nurse clinician to carry on this work.

Regular classes for nursing staff are well attended. An additional and unanticipated result of these new techniques in dealing with children has been their effect on the morale of the nurses themselves. Involvement in the program has brought about closer working relationships, greater support of staff members for one another, and a new enthusiasm for patient care. Parents have also shown appreciation of the individualized care their children receive, and this is rewarding for the staff.

One young nurse on the floor stated her feelings quite frankly.

I was trained in school to know that the children need support and that it is important to understand their emotional and developmental needs. When I first went into a hospital—not this one—I was trying to give a little individual attention to each child I took care of. Then I caught *that look* on the faces of nurses who were already experienced. I think every young nurse knows that look. It means, "Here's little Florence Nightingale trying to be everybody's angel of mercy. Well, she'll get over it. Wait until she's been here a while!" It made me feel like a fool—I was embarrassed to be seen playing with the babies or trying to be friendly with them. That's why I like to work here; you can be a person and treat the children as human beings. We all learned in training that it's important to do that, but if nobody helps you with it or encourages you to do it, then it's very hard to be anything more than a technician.

Many of the nurses agree that they were encouraged to participate in these more personal ways of relating to children by actually seeing the techniques demonstrated and by seeing the results. They also found the discussions and conferences of great value in dealing with the patient's problem and with their own feelings.

Miss Petrillo adds her own conviction that one important facet of success has been the gradual introduction of the program. She has great respect for the dedication and expertise of the nursing profession and feels strongly that any such program can be introduced only as an aid to and an enrichment of nursing and not as a superimposed series of absolutes.

New York Hospital-Cornell Medical Center now has mimeographed sheets of instructions and information for parents whose children come in for tonsillectomy or eye surgery. They have, as well, an admission booklet for all children, brightly illustrated in several colors, with an introductory page for parents. There is a clear map of the floors the family will enter, with the main and emergency entrances marked. The booklet is printed in two languages, English and Spanish.

The role of Miss Petrillo as special liaison, or ombudsman, illustrates the way in which a change in attitude and more rewarding relationships can be brought about. From a position which was at first looked upon with a lack of understanding and sometimes resentment or suspicion by a majority of the staff, she was able to make her skills available in a manner that was practical and useful to nurses and patients alike. Without imposing more than was acceptable, or moving at a rate which put pressure on nurses to assume a role in which they did not feel comfortable, she brought new concepts into pediatrics. That these concepts, and the way they are currently in use, is rewarding for staff, parents, and children is amply demonstrated by the fact that they are now an integral part of nursing at New York Hospital-Cornell Medical Center and by the fact that the nursing administration has approved three positions for mental health nursing personnel in pediatrics alone.

PARENT-CHILD ADVOCATES IN NURSING

Three liaison positions in other hospitals similar in many respects to those previously discussed are held by Mrs. Edith Amend of Children's Hospital of Philadelphia, Mrs. Polly Hesterberg of The Johns Hopkins Hospital Children's Medical and Surgical Center, and Mrs. Caroline Overfors of the Children's Hospital Medical Center of Boston. Mrs. Hesterberg of The Johns Hopkins Hospital is primarily concerned directly with parents. As Living-In Coordinator, she interviews parents individually and leads their discussion groups; she also meets with staff members and outside community groups. Her role combines autonomy of judgment and interaction with all the services dealing with the family as well as the child: social service, visiting nurses, and the public relations department, which supplies volunteer jobs for parents who make a prolonged stay. Her role with parents who live in has been discussed in Chapter 3. Mrs. Amend at Children's Hospital of Philadelphia, whose position has also been detailed previously, is chiefly concerned with parents, although she prepares mothers and children together for the child's surgery and follows up this preparation with visits to the child on the unit and with cooperation with the anesthesiologist. Since Children's Hospital of Philadelphia has limited accommodations for parents, her information and help differ in detail but not in essential philosophy from those of Mrs. Hesterberg.

A third special position of this kind is that of Mrs. Caroline Overfors, Coordinator of Parent Education at Children's Hospital Medical Center of Boston. Her role is different from that of the other two, in that information and reassurance about living in are not her function since the Medical Center does not have a structured policy of living in. She counsels parents and acts as liaison between the surgical staff and the family. Her chief contacts are with parents of children scheduled for surgery or children in the Intensive Care Unit. Less actively involved with children on the units than Mrs. Hesterberg and Mrs. Amend, she nevertheless has a similar function in calling on other departments such as social services when they can be helpful. She is in close contact with the operating room in order to give the parents information about the child's condition. She is also available to parents at home and can be easily reached by telephone.

These three positions are held by registered nurses, all of whom consider their nursing experience a valuable asset since many of the parents' questions are directed toward the child's condition and details of nursing care. Mrs. Hesterberg and Mrs. Overfors wear uniforms, Mrs. Amend wears daytime dresses.

Mrs. Hesterberg's position was created as a part of the living-in policy, which has been an integral part of The Johns Hopkins Hospital Children's Medical and Surgical Center since the new facility was opened. Mrs. Overfors' position was initially requested by Dr. T. Berry Brazelton, who joined the staff of Children's Hospital Medical Center of Boston in 1968. It was filled by the Department of Nursing. Mrs. Amend's position, unlike the other two, was initiated by the director of nursing at Children's Hospital of Philadelphia and not by the medical staff. The Department of Nursing here works very closely with the Children's Activities Program, and Mrs. Amend has close and informal relationships with both. The definition of her job, its goals, and the ways in which she makes it effective were largely dictated by her own initiative. For this she has both respect and praise for the director of nursing to whom she is responsible. "We were really pioneering in this job, and Miss Rothrock told me to go ahead and to do what I thought was necessary and right. I talked to nurses and asked them if they had any special requests for help. The ear, nose, and throat staff seemed to have the most immediate need, so I began to counsel those mothers individually. Sometimes there were misunderstandings because I went everywhere in the hospital and wasn't subject to the usual nursing rules, but Miss Rothrock always supported what I was doing and gave me the authority to go ahead. Now that my job is better understood, nurses do call on me for help and rely on what I can do.

Less important than the differences between these positions are the factors they have in common: they were all initiated specifically for meeting the needs of families in new ways, they are all engaged in exploring new techniques and in opening new avenues of communication, and they all exist because someone in authority was aware of the actual existence of parents. In many conventional hospitals parents are thought of in the abstract—even though they are physically present, they are often dealt with as a sort of generalization. In one such hospital, no member of the nursing staff approached a Navajo father and mother who sat silently beside their child's bed. Only when a volunteer who spoke Navajo had greeted the couple on her own initiative did the staff find that these parents spoke fluent English but had been too intimidated to ask help from the forbidding figures in white. They had waited, without a break, a cup of coffee, or a glance from anyone who went by, for more than four hours in the hope that the doctor might come.

Daily census-taking, scheduling, and shortages of staff mean little to parents who are personally and vitally concerned with the welfare of a single child. Until their immediate anxiety is relieved and they are able to trust those around them, they are less capable of objectivity about hospital rules and timetables than at any other time. A sympathetic human being, competent to answer routine questions and sensitive enough to see families as individuals, can often solve the small misunderstandings that could grow into major difficulties and can smooth the way for families and staff alike.

These liaison positions were all created to bring about better understanding between the hospital and the parent; although they differ in scope, degree, and detail, they are all significant in that they are indications of the growing awareness in forward-looking hospitals that technology cannot replace human relationships.

REFERENCES

Coyle, G., and Fisher, R. Helping hospitalized children through social group work. *The Child* 16:114, 1952.

Langford, W. Physical illness and convalescence: Their meaning to the child. *Journal of Pediatrics* 33:242-250, 1948.

Langford, W. The child in pediatric hospital: Adaptation to illness and hospitalization. *American Journal of Orthopsychiatry* 31:667-684, 1961.

Petrillo, M. Preventing hospital trauma in pediatric patients. *American Journal of Nursing* 68:1468, 1968.

Plank, E. N. Death on a children's ward. *Medical Times* 92:638-644, 1964.

Prugh, D. G., Staub, E. M., Sands, H. H., Kirschbaum, R. M., and Lenihan, E. A. A study of the emotional reactions of children and families to hospitalization and illness. *American Journal of Orthopsychiatry* 23:70-106, 1953.

Scahill, M. Preparing children for procedures and operations. *Nursing Outlook,* June 1969. P. 36.

Shore, M. F. (Ed.). *Red Is the Color of Hurting.* Bethesda, Md.: National Institute of Mental Health, 1967.

Shore, M. F., Glisser, R. L., and Walman, H. M.   Constructive uses of a hospital experience. *Children* 12:3-8, 1965.

Tisza, V. B. The management of the chronically ill child. *American Journal of Orthopsychiatry* 32:53-59, 1962.

Tisza, V. B., and Angoff, K.   A play program and its function in pediatric hospital. *Pediatrics* 19:293, 1957.

Tisza, V. B., and Angoff, K.   A play program for hospitalized children: The role of the playroom teacher. *Pediatrics* 28:841, 1961.

6

Hospitals and Their Communities

ALMOST no hospital today can be said to treat only the patients within its walls. Outpatient departments, social services, links with medical schools, research programs, and satellite clinics are the rule rather than the exception. However, the ways in which hospital administrations perceive the communities around them can influence how patients make use of services as well as the quality of care.

"One reason for having a parent stay with a child," according to one head nurse on a large pediatric ward, "is that when the parent is here, the child gets better care. It is frightening but true that a child who seems utterly alone, with nobody from outside showing personal concern for him, can become a laboratory for the doctors. They can forget he's human and use him as a teaching device or as a clinical guinea pig with no regard for what he's feeling or thinking. A child can suffer from unnecessary procedures simply because the doctor is interested in a medical specialty, or suffer emotional damage because he is at everyone's mercy and yet nobody takes more than a passing interest in him as a person."

"Parents visit here at any time of the day or night. We have had parents at four o'clock in the morning, fathers coming off a late work shift," says one director of nursing. "If a procedure is going on and they can get an explanation, they're reassured. If the child is playing or asleep, they can see for themselves that he's all right. Trust is one of our keystones for good care."

Untrustworthiness and frightening secrecy are sometimes unwittingly communicated to the child and his family even before they reach the pediatric unit. Interminable waits, brusque voices giving directions, complicated and bewildering information forms, omnipotence, and lack of personal interest convey the message of the family's diminished status and perhaps even its culpability in having allowed the child to become sick.

Some hospitals, very much aware of this problem of detachment from and lack of respect for the human beings they serve, are looking to the communities around them and reevaluating their own responsibilities as educators and purveyors of preventive health care. They are moving beyond the old image of sterile isolation into a new role of responsive interaction, one in which hospital staff and community augment each other's contribution to the health of the children.

HUNTERDON MEDICAL CENTER

One hospital which may be unique in the country in this respect is the Hunterdon Medical Center in Flemington, New Jersey. From its inception, Hunterdon has been a community project, closely linked with the population around it. A comparatively small center of 156 beds, it has an effectiveness in the area disproportionate to its size. The history of how it came into being is the key to its present policies and to its position in the rural community it serves.

In the 1940's, at the end of World War II, Hunterdon County, an agricultural area with a low-income, sparsely distributed population, had no hospital and no medical specialists. There were 32 general practitioners in the county, of whom 14 had no affiliations or courtesy privileges with any hospital. The average family income was the lowest of any county in New Jersey, and infant mortality and death rates were higher than state averages.

The County Board of Agriculture, an important central body and community forum for the agricultural population, was concerned about the lack of health care and in 1946 appointed a committee to survey the medical needs and facilities of the county. The result of the study was a series of prolonged public debates and open hearings, which lasted for more than three years. A fund-raising campaign was begun in 1949, by which time the entire county was concerned and involved, having had ample opportunity to discuss every aspect of need, financing, and construction. Almost every family contributed to the hospital campaign (one newspaper headline at the time read, "Cow Yields $162.80 for Medical Center"). In addition to extensive and dedicated fund-raising, the county eventually also obtained grants from the federal Hill-Burton Program and from the New Jersey Commonwealth Fund.

The Hunterdon Medical Center opened in 1953 and has since expanded its facilities. It stands in open country on the outskirts of Flemington, surrounded by rolling meadows and trees. Inside, it is both efficient and pleasant, with soft colors, unobtrusive lighting, and a general air of informality.

Special facilities for orthopedics, speech therapy, the monitoring of heart patients in an intensive care unit, and x-ray are included. It has links of varying degrees with five medical schools outside the county.

Excellent as its facilities are, its real significance lies in its policies and community relations. Because the community actively participated in the planning and fund-raising and because the medical and administrative staff were committed from the beginning to the concept of a true center of medicine, in the sense of a central unit that would concern itself with all aspects of health in the county, some policies of Hunterdon Medical Center today are markedly different from those of the usual hospital.

A staff specialist heads each hospital service. As a condition of employment, each must be connected with a university faculty, and each is expected to spend at least one day a week in teaching or research at his university. These specialists (they do not engage in outside practice) have offices and secretaries at the hospital and are on salary. Standard fees are charged for formal consultations and referrals and from patients who consult the doctors directly. These fees go into a professional fund administered by the center for the salaries and office expenses of the specialist staff.

Only staff specialists may perform surgery. Each is responsible for the quality of care given the patient in his specialty, even if the patient is hospitalized by an outside doctor without previous consultation or reference to the specialist. A staff internist routinely makes rounds and studies each patient.

What, then, is the role of the family doctor? The center considers him a vital partner with the specialist staff in patient care, since he has knowledge of the patient's family and background and the ability to follow up the patient after hospitalization. Although the staff specialist is the only doctor permitted to do surgery, the family doctor may assist, and his continuing involvement assures that comprehensive and total care will continue and that the specialist will have his proper role—that of dealing with a particular area of expertise.

"Fragmentation" of the patient, particularly of children and of geriatric patients, both of whom are least able to communicate their needs, is a common problem in many hospitals. Interactions with a child's family and an awareness of the total context in which the patient leads his life are often ignored in large and overworked wards because the specialists are concerned with their particular field and other staff personnel are too busy. At the center the child's doctor has a continuing relationship with the family and can take many pertinent factors into consideration, while the specialist has his in-depth and particular knowledge to contribute. Since the child does not change doctors to become the patient of the specialist, family doctors are not reluctant to make referrals and specialists are able to give their best medical and surgical efforts. There is a remarkable cooperation among doctors at Hunterdon; professional rivalries seem to be minimal.

But the center's policy extends beyond this unusual mutual respect between medical professionals. From the beginning, Hunterdon Medical Center has been concerned with coordinating many services, with a constant awareness of the county's needs. Dr. Avrum Katcher, director of pediatrics, outlines the relationship of the hospital to the community, particularly that part dealing with pediatrics.

The institution should exist as an integrated therapeutic community. The child patient is always a part of his family constellation and of his surrounding community. So the relationship, instead of being a single and fragmented thing, should be a relationship between the whole hospital in all its complexity, the whole family, and the whole community. The hospital becomes the doctor, the family becomes the patient, the community is an entity involved with the two. For part of the total well-being of the family, perhaps the hospital social worker is communicating with a parent; for the immediate medical care, the physician is communicating with the child. But the child and the parent are still linked, and we cannot deal with each in a separate compartment. Who best meets the need? Who needs the support at this time? These are the questions we have to ask, and then the appropriate things are done. If the child can stay at home where he feels less threatened by illness, and if our help can support the mother and make it easier for her to take care of the child, then our efforts should be directed there. If the visit of a social worker or nurse can supply the help the family needs, then she is the key person for the time she is needed. It doesn't always have to be the traditional dialogue; we have to change as the factors change. There are all sorts of networks we can utilize; there are many supportive influences that can be helpful.

The center has close links with the Visiting Nurses Association and with the Homemaker Service, both of which have offices on the hospital grounds. The liaison is carried out by a medical center committee that checks on cases and makes special medical care available from the hospital if needed. A speech therapy program in the county schools is staffed by therapists from the center who also consult with the center's pediatric and psychiatric staff. With this as its operative policy, it is not surprising that the center has involved entire families in its patient care from the beginning.

The 20-bed pediatric unit is adjacent to the obstetric unit. The atmosphere is lively and informal, and a waiting area has comfortable chairs and a coffee table. A playroom at the end of the unit is equipped with sturdy toys and equipment. Parents are not considered visitors; they are always welcome. In the obstetric section fathers come in at all times to see their wives and babies. The obstetric department from the beginning offered parent-education classes for mothers and fathers and allowed mothers to room in with infants. This policy is so much a matter of the mother's readiness and choice that babies may often spend a few hours with their mothers, then a time in the nursery while the mothers sleep or see visitors, and then go back to the mothers again. Eight of the obstetric section's 10 rooms are 2-bed units. As a rule, in a 2-bed unit both mothers have their babies with them; the staff feels it is often an encouragement to a mother who is unsure of herself to see that her roommate has her baby nearby. "Then she wants to boast a little about her baby, too. And she sees that it's easy to have the baby there." However, a mother is not urged to have the baby with her if she feels insecure.

Fathers are shown the technique of washing up and are given gowns. After these precautions, they may feed their babies or even learn to change diapers. There are classes with demonstrations for the mothers, who sometimes bathe their babies at the bedside under a nurse's supervision, with fathers occasionally helping with the bath. Seventy percent of the husbands are present in the labor and delivery rooms; they have never been a source of contagion and their presence is of real value.

"We show them which wall to lean against, and how to slide down if they feel faint," an obstetric nurse says. "But only three fathers have fainted in the last nine years. Fathers are really a help to the wives. Families get such a feeling of being together when they see their own baby being born."

Mothers are encouraged to breast-feed their babies but are

not pressed to do so if they appear reluctant; about 44 percent of the mothers do breast-feed their infants. A booklet given to pregnant mothers on admission gives detailed and reassuring information on newborns, with the information directed to the father as well as the mother. Appropriately called *And Baby Makes Three—Or So,* it demonstrates the center's emphasis on the total family.

The admission booklet for the pediatric department, with an introduction by Dr. Katcher, states in part: "Sick children are often afraid and lonely. If your child needs you at his side you are welcome to stay as long as necessary. We'll see that you have a bed. We're delighted if you show us the special ways of doing things your child prefers." This booklet gives the geographic locations of the rooms the parents may use and the daily routine of the 20-bed unit—16 children's beds and 4 for adolescents. It outlines the procedure of staying overnight with the child (using a cot which the hospital provides without charge), and it encourages the parent to enter into the routine of bathing and feeding the child as much as possible. Here again, the policy of the hospital is indicated by the title of the pamphlet: *When Your Child is in Pediatrics—What You Can Do to Help.* (The word *You* stands out in a separate color from the rest of the lettering.)

Parents may visit at all times; other visitors are limited to afternoons, and children under 12 are not allowed. But the policy is even more flexible than the pamphlet would indicate since the staff believes in adjusting to the needs of individual families.

An hour on the pediatric and obstetric floor is the best indication of the kind of flexibility that the center practices in pediatrics and of the way in which it carries out the policies expressed in the information booklets.

A voice from a room in the obstetric unit calls out, "Is a

nurse out there? Will somebody tell someone to come in here?" Within minutes a nurse has gone into the room and there is a dialogue punctuated with the laughter of several voices. As the nurse reappears, she sees visitors in the small waiting area.

"It's a bore, waiting. I'll bring you a cup of coffee," she says cheerfully. She reappears shortly, delivers the coffee, and vanishes again into the patient's room. A mother, carrying a lunch tray from the coffee shop downstairs, emerges from the elevator and goes down the hall to the playroom. From a playpen set up by the nurses' desk, two soft toys are hurled to the floor. The nurse at the desk leans over to the baby girl in the playpen.

"Couldn't you keep them in there for five minutes? I don't know what I'm going to do with you," she says with patient indulgence. A young Candy Striper returns the toys. "Oh, *you*. I know what *you're* up to," she tells the baby.

"Will you go see Lenore?" the nurse asks the volunteer. "She's all right, but she's cross. Just read to her or talk. It's so uncomfortable now that those burns are healing, and she's sick of being cooped up."

A toy comes flying out of the playpen again. "She likes being out here where there's company, but she takes a lot of picking up after," the head nurse says resignedly.

In the playroom the mother with the tray is eating lunch with her little boy, who has his tray on a play table. His lunch had been delayed while he had some tests.

"Can I give him a little of this?" the mother asks the nurse.

"Yes, that's all right," says the nurse. "Yours looks better to him than his, doesn't it? That's always the way."

A mother and father are talking in low tones in the hall. Another mother comes quickly out of a room and crosses to the nurses' desk.

"She says it itches and she wants me to rub some Vaseline on it," she tells the nurse at the desk. "She's so fussy—I don't know what to do with her."

The nurse reaches casually for a tube of Vaseline and hands it over the desk. "You might as well rub on a little. It won't do any harm, and it might make her feel better if she thinks you're doing something for her."

"Thanks," says the mother fervently, and vanishes.

"I don't know . . ." says the nurse absently, going back to her charts. "It might even make it feel better, at that . . ."

All these interactions are low-keyed and casual. There are empty beds in some rooms; sometimes the pediatric unit may have only half its beds occupied. Dr. Katcher's criteria for admission are three: (1) if the parent's coping mechanisms are overwhelmed at the moment; (2) if the physician's resources for handling the patient at home are insufficient; and (3) the smallest category of the three, if there is a real need for the special facilities which can be found only in the hospital. He believes that a sick child should not be hospitalized just because it is the easiest routine way of dealing with illness. In the same way, although hospital policy is one of cooperation with the parents in the care of the child, he is not a rigid adherent of the theory that the mother's presence is invariably necessary to the child's well-being. Adaptability of policy to individuals is the pediatric policy.

"People who work here," says Dr. Katcher, "must know one another's skills sufficiently well so that any may speak for the integrated community. When the nurse relates to the patient around a specific task, such as dispensing a medication, she steps out of the institutional unit and establishes a relationship with the child for that purpose. She represents, or comes with, the goodwill of the total institution. Five minutes later, an attendant, who perhaps lives near the parents, may be talking to the father and their conversation will be partly social and partly about medical care. The father may say something highly relevant to the health care process, a point of information, for example, which the attendant will report back to the nurse or doctor. A significant relationship may occur through someone else entirely. Therefore, within the basic element, which is institution and family, relationships may shift. Data may be acquired by any one of a number of different routes. Intervention, in terms of the influence of the medical care system upon the child and family, may also be made a number of different ways."

As an example of this flexible use of data and of relationships, Dr. Katcher cites the case of a child who needed speech therapy after being discharged from the hospital. He attended a school which was not equipped to give him this help, but in the course of an unrelated informal conversation, his attending doctor learned that a skilled speech therapist lived in the child's neighborhood. One telephone call to this therapist was all that was needed to arrange for the child to receive adequate help outside school hours.

Dr. Katcher believes in choosing the course for getting data, or intervening, that is most suitable to the task at hand, whether or not it is a traditional one. "But you don't go out of your way to utilize a nontraditional route," he adds, "unless it really offers you something. Medical histories and physical examinations are still important."

Hunterdon Medical Center now draws its patient load from an area of about six counties—that is, from a travel-time radius of only about one and a half hours. Thus, although some families stay overnight (as the admission booklet invites them to do) most parents live so close that it is more practical and desirable for them to go home. Staying for many days with a child in the busy and noisy atmosphere of the hospital can be hard on mothers, particularly those with many family obligations. The flexible attitude of the staff is notable in the variety of arrangements made to help mothers in this situation.

A grandmother or other family member may stay if it seems more supportive for the child; a child may do better with a hospital worker than with any family member, depending on the circumstances at home and on the illness. The Visiting Nurses Association and the Homemaker Service have a close association with the hospital; their services are paid for under the patient's hospitalization plan, and he is still carried on the hospital rolls while he is in need of these home services. Estimates have shown that a child can be cared for at home for three days with these services for approximately the same cost to the family as one day in an acute-care bed.

The center is host to a constant stream of visitors who come from other institutions to study its policies and their implementation. A typical sidelight on the pediatric section is that about once a year it allows boy and girl scout troops to visit, the kind of invasion of outside children that would be unthinkable in many institutions. The children take delight, on the visit, in pointing out familiar landmarks from previous hospitalizations of their own, or in telling about a sibling or friend who was in the pediatric unit. The staff looks upon the visit as a time for allaying children's fears about the hospital and for explaining hospital rules and the reasons for them, as a preparation for possible later hospitalizations as well as for dealing with the misconceptions and myths that often confuse children's thinking.

Both the professionals and the scout troop visitors may

well find that a visit one year later will show innovations. The specialist staff with their continuing relationships with the universities, the population around the hospital with its expanding needs and changing ideas, the family doctors in the area, some of whom trained at the center, all have interactions with the hospital, which is responsive to feedback at many different levels and meets changes with flexible policies.

It has sometimes been said that the center was fortunate in having been founded in an area lacking organized medical care. Without any previous medical hierarchy resistant to change, with a new field for endeavor, and with a demonstrated need for medical service, the original staff was able to establish a center in which the specialist and the general practitioner could work together with a minimum of traditional rivalry and in which the community could feel itself a partner in the enterprise from the beginning. However, fortunate as it may have been in these respects, there is one fact that emerges as the most significant: many new hospitals have been built since Hunterdon Medical Center, but few, if any, have listened so carefully to the individual voices in the community and responded so totally, and few give such respect and equality to all professionals—specialist, family doctor, nurses, and workers in the social services.

THE JOHNS HOPKINS HOSPITAL

Physically different in almost every way possible from Hunterdon Medical Center is The Johns Hopkins Hospital in Baltimore. It is surrounded by a deteriorated red-brick ghetto that houses a low-income, largely minority population.

Patients come from this area as well as from every state and many foreign countries. Since it opened in 1889, endowed by private funds, the hospital has expanded its facilities until it now has more than 1,000 beds and its buildings are spread over fourteen urban acres. The long-established position of the hospital as a separate island in the city blocks that stretch around it and the very size of the staff of several hundred doctors, as well as the nursing, social work and therapy staffs, and other personnel, would seem to preclude any personal and individualized commitment to the community outside its doors. However, the pediatric department here carries out a policy of total concern with individual children and their families that is among the most forward-looking in the country. The implementation of the policy in the inpatient pediatric units has been discussed elsewhere (Chapter 3).

There are many pediatric specialty clinics at The Johns Hopkins Hospital, as well as the general outpatient clinic. The Child Life Department staff, which serves all pediatrics, has conducted activities programs in these clinics since 1961. But it is another activity of the Child Life Department, one which brings the hospital directly into contact with the community around it, that adds another dimension to the usual child care role of such an institution. To clarify how this new link with the ghetto surrounding the hospital came about, and to appreciate the work of the Family Life Department staff who are responsible for carrying it out, one must first understand the hospital's Comprehensive Child Care Program and the associated part played in it by the Child Life Department.

Comprehensive Child Care is a program funded by a federal grant for the delivery of health care to the well child. It is carried out by the hospital through the use of its own medical facilities and special paramedical services and through cooperation with schools and outside health service agencies. More than 22,000 children in areas adjacent to the hospital are eligible for this program, and a large proportion of them are enrolled in it. The Comprehensive Child Care Clinic in the hospital, under the direction of Dr. Robert Cooke, became increasingly concerned several years ago about the conditions to which inpatient and clinic children returned after care in the hospital, and particularly after clinic visits. As part of their involvement with all aspects of pediatrics, and given impetus by the concern of Dr. Cooke, the Child Life Department undertook a study of the recreational-educational facilities, professional supervision, and care at home in several small adjacent ghetto neighborhoods. The study was followed by a demonstration of community needs carried out by high school students in a summer recreational program. The results of these investigations showed the community pathology and need for facilities of all kinds to be great; the area surrounding the hospital is a potentially explosive one in many ways since its low-income, minority population is badly overcrowded and inadequately housed.

The post of Family Life Coordinator was created in 1968 to produce new ways to meet these needs. Mr. Lewis Gwynn, Jr., who has filled the position since its inception, is also an associate director of the Child Life Department. The outlines of his job are broad in scope; his area of involvement is child life in the community, although he works in and through the hospital. "We hope basically," he says, "to make ourselves available to children and parents in the community, to work for the child and with the world around him through local organizations, his family and friends, his educational and play areas. Then we want to follow up after he's been in the hospital, to go back into his community and help with problems that arise there and cause return trips to the hospital. We have access to all kinds of research and technology furnished by the hospital professionals—the drug-abuse program, psychological studies, and many other resources—that we can use to help families and neighborhoods."

One way to facilitate this relationship between the hospital and the surrounding area is to use the existing organizations and concerned groups in the census tracts adjacent to the hospital. Mr. Gwynn started to make contact with these groups in the most direct and informal way—by going into the neighborhood and talking to people in their own clubs, churches, and organizations, in their homes, and on the streets. But even with the advantage of familiarity with the area and the people, he found himself faced with distrust and lack of confidence because of his hospital association. This was overcome "by showing them that I'm not an expert. Nobody's an expert—we don't even know all the problems. But whatever information we had that might be helpful to them, I offered to them." Mothers concerned with starting day-care groups and families who wanted play areas and after-school programs for their children found him willing and helpful in writing proposals; families concerned with the special needs of individual children learned that he had access to resources they could use. As the community gradually began to trust him, and as they learned that he was never aligned with any political faction ("I wouldn't take a stand on either side because I was just there for the children."), the people of the community began to use him more and more as a consultant and to come to him for help with problems.

Although this position has existed less than 5 years, the results have been remarkable. Mr. Gwynn has established a community center of communication within the hospital itself. People from the surrounding area come to his office to hold discussions, to consult individually, and to form groups concerned with a particular child-oriented project. In the community, he sits with church boards to help them fund programs in their own churches, on the Citizens Council for Day Care and Recreation for the City of Baltimore, and on the Maryland Committee for Social Welfare (Children's Division).

Currently, he is training a group of local high school seniors as Family Life Assistants. Funded by the Office of Economic Opportunity and aided by a speech therapist and a graduate in home economics, he gives his students one hour a day of work-study in the hospital and additional paid job training either in ward playrooms or in the community. This National Youth Council Child Life Trainee Program was initiated by Mrs. Barbara Haas, then director of the Child Life Department. With Mr. Gwynn, she began with a group of high school dropouts and seniors who were potential school dropouts. For the first few months the program was met with minimal response. During the following summer, however, when the program had been in operation for about six to nine months, the Family Life Assistants, under supervision, brought quality recreation and meaningful activities to more than 1,500 neglected children in the area, who otherwise would have had no summer programs. Recreation in local neighborhoods, and a special educational effort that caused many children to be registered in the clinic for the first time, were part of a highly successful introduction to better care in the neighborhoods and, at the same time, to training the Family Life Assistants to deal with core community problems.

This direct involvement on a local neighborhood level is the key to Mr. Gwynn's policy: the use of resources near at hand and the education of families to help solve problems within their own neighborhoods. Many resources already exist within a community which need only some service-oriented professional help or some access to information to make them effective. Outsiders, even skilled ones, sometimes make social and psychological blunders which impede individual and group progress simply because they may be unaware of the existing culture or attitudes. Mr. Gwynn has given impetus to two leisure-time programs in local churches that are carried out in the evenings; they are oriented to help the entire family, with recreation, remedial education, and health services which can lead back to the services of the clinic. The churches also have day-care programs which, by involving parents and children together, can bring to light problems that might otherwise pass unnoticed.

"We have a Parents' Advisory Council now," says Mr. Gwynn, "which meets on Saturdays. One of the members' new ideas is to do volunteer work in our clinic one or two days a week. They could help with the child care program while learning something about child development and good health care at the same time. I meet with the Parents' Advisory Council to help with their very successful news-letter, which goes out to the families of clinic patients. It reaches about nine thousand families."

A typical example of the way in which a community potential can be developed was a program based in a church near The Johns Hopkins Hospital and already funded by a community agency to include about 70 children from 4 to 12 years old. Although it could draw on donations of supplies and of milk and cookies from several sources, it was in danger of becoming ineffective because of misunder-standings among staff members. By listening to the problems and taking time to befriend the program, Mr. Gwynn's staff was able to resolve some of the difficulties, and the program, with new enthusiasm, now involves both parents and children in education and recreation, arts and crafts projects, and a summer camping facility. It also supplies a health and medical service and a library.

Mr. Gwynn also acts as liaison between the hospital and the community by participating in the work of Fellowship House, a multipurpose human relations center that has been active since the 1940's and which draws its membership from every part of Baltimore. Here he finds valuable contacts between interracial groups and an opportunity to coordinate efforts, which otherwise might be fragmented, to supply health and education services to minority group children.

A very important part of the position of Family Life Coordinator, he is convinced, is his communication with medical staff and social service personnel within the hospital itself. Because the medical institution is large and complex, and because its personnel includes many people from various backgrounds as well as students from abroad, he finds that there are areas of unawareness among personnel about the lives of local patients, their home situations, and even the conditions of the streets, housing, and sanitation to which they will be returned after discharge from the wards.

"I'm constantly meeting with hospital staff people, talking, discussing—sometimes with reports or proposals, sometimes with films we have made in the community following the community children as they develop, showing what they do and the kind of environment they live in. This office is always open for use as a resource for information. I find the hospital staff tends to use it more and more. I'm trying to bridge a gap between people and between groups."

Mr. Gwynn is now working with a Child Care Improvement Committee, in conjunction with the mayor's office, on a city-wide basis. He has also now begun speaking in other parts of the state.

In a ghetto area like the one surrounding the magnificent

new buildings of the hospital and the traditional red brick of the original building, visual contrasts are very noticeable. The underlying lack of communication, the strong emotional reactions lying close beneath the surface, are still in evidence, and many cannot be solved or dealt with easily or in a short time. While they wait for solutions, the crowds continue to pour into The Johns Hopkins Hospital from every state and country; they fill the halls with the surf-sound of thousands of moving feet, wait for elevators filled to capacity, and are directed by tireless hostesses at information desks. At the same time, the medical staff, nurses, aides, therapists, students, and Child Life Department workers continue to try to meet difficult schedules and heavy caseloads. Almost everyone in a professional capacity in the hospital will speak of the need for more space, more time, more professionals. Lewis Gwynn, driving through the surrounding run-down streets, points to an empty building, "We could use that for a child care program if we could get the funding."

The remarkable and heartening fact is that despite all these problems and inconveniences, and without sacrificing its research and training programs or its standard of superior care, the pediatric department has made the transition from the traditional role of dispenser of care and unassailable authority to partner in care and participating member of its own community.

CHILDREN'S HOSPITAL OF PHILADELPHIA

Other large hospitals in many cities are beginning to reorganize their outpatient clinics to meet community needs similar to those surrounding The Johns Hopkins Hospital. Indicative of the kind of new thinking emerging in urban areas is a federally funded program in Philadelphia, which involves five medical schools in a coordinated attempt to bring better health care to communities within the city. Under a coordinating executive board which includes public health and school representatives, five medical schools have set up five clinics in Philadelphia which will pool their research and evaluations to carry out community care in target areas. Basically a community service project, each also collects data on its own effectiveness, on community needs, and on operational costs.

The clinic carrying out this program at the Children's Hospital of Philadelphia, Operation Rebound, is typical of the way in which the service is structured to serve an individual area. Operation Rebound, set up in 1966, is centered on a single target area of about 530 families within walking distance of the hospital. It is housed in a small building adjacent to the hospital proper but makes use of hospital services.

The criteria of eligibility for the clinic service are geographic location and patient age: all patients must come from the target area, and the age limitation is from 1 day to 14 years. The hospital provides staff for the clinic, and the chief of pediatrics of the hospital, also on the faculty of The University of Pennsylvania School of Medicine, provides leadership for the clinic as well as a close link with the hospital.

The structure of the clinic is like that of a private practice group. Teams, which include the doctor, nurse, dentist, and social worker, have an ongoing, continuous relationship with each family. The family sees the same personnel at each visit and is thus able to build familiarity and trust with them in the same way that a family at a higher income level relates to a family doctor. After clinic hours, the hospital telephone operator takes clinic emergency calls and attempts to get in touch with the physician who has been assigned to the family. Study of the families using the Operation Rebound facility indicate that 80 percent very much prefer this system to the more usual clinic arrangement in which families see an available staff doctor—often a different one each time that they visit.

One effect of the team approach in the clinic has been the new peer relationship which has developed within the professional staff. Team conferences have led to a more autonomous role for nurses, with more equality of status with the medical staff since the nurses' evaluations of and relationships with families can contribute importantly to team knowledge.

"We find that people often think in terms of stereotypes of doctor, dentist, and nurse," says Dr. E. Peter Wilson, director of the clinic. "In a group like this in which all contributions are of equal importance and good communication and teamwork are a necessity, we are getting rid of stereotypes. With the facilities of the hospital available and staffed as we are, we can do anything for a family that a group of doctors in private practice can do."

As a part of the community, Operation Rebound works with the schools in conjunction with school nurses, and it recruits some of its social workers directly from the target area for closer liaison with the families of the neighborhood. The clinic has been in operation for less than six years and is still in the process of evaluating its own services and collecting research data.

NEW YORK HOSPITAL-CORNELL MEDICAL CENTER

A similar clinic restructuring is under way in New York, where the New York Hospital-Cornell Medical Center is setting up four clinic teams similar to Operation Rebound to care for patients, with particular families seeing "their own" doctors on a continuing basis. The four team divisions have been given the names of flowers—Azalea, Begonia, Carnation, Daisy—in order to make them easier for families to remember and identify. This has been found particularly helpful to those families who speak imperfect English or are only partially literate.

In the short time that the new team plan has been in operation there has been evidence that, although the problem of broken appointments common to all clinics has not been appreciably bettered, there are more telephone calls to notify the clinic that a patient will not keep an appointment. The staff is encouraged by this indication of patient obligation to the clinic to believe that the attitude of families toward a team with whom they can become familiar will encourage the keeping of appointments and thus will lead to better health care.

Operation Rebound and the clinic at the New York Hospital-Cornell Medical Center are indicative of a growing awareness that the patient's family and background are key factors in ongoing health care. Satellite clinics in other cities are reorganizing parts of their staff into similar cooperative teams to give families a continuing relationship with a single group of medical workers with whom they can communicate more readily.

CLEVELAND   METROPOLITAN   GENERAL HOSPITAL

At Cleveland Metropolitan General Hospital, the out-patient clinic playroom is used to generate this kind of trust and communication. It is worth attention here because within the structure of a conventional clinic this playroom has multiple functions reaching beyond the primary one of keeping children amused and occupied while waiting for appointments.

The pediatric outpatient clinic handles as many as 150 patients a day and has 11 examining and treatment rooms. The playroom is supervised by Miss Wilma Rice under the direction of Mrs. Emma Plank, director of the Child Life and Education Department. Miss Rice is assisted during the mornings by two high school seniors on a work-study program and by college students during other hours.

The playroom is a large, open area separated from the parents' waiting area by a low wall of book and toy shelves. It is adjacent to some of the examining rooms, which are separated from it only by curtains and are brightened by mobiles and wall decorations supplied by the playroom staff. Children frequently look in these rooms and play near them, familiarizing themselves in an informal way with the medical setting. Even the occasional loud crying of a child behind drawn curtains does not seem to cause undue anxiety.

The parents' waiting area is supplied with pamphlets on child care and development and other magazines, and there are nutrition charts on the wall. It is so close to the play area that the children come and go informally, sometimes bringing their mothers into the play area.

Miss Rice sees the whole pediatric clinic as her area of concern. She uses the playroom to observe children's reactions and may make entries on their charts or on occasion consult with the pediatricians and nurses. She is sensitive to clues from the mothers about the home situation and can often reassure them and help them in understanding the day-to-day needs of children. She can consult social workers and make recommendations to them on the basis of her friendship with the family.

There are opportunities here in the playroom for parents to see their children display skills and qualities of which they might not have been aware. Miss Rice tries to assure an atmosphere of freedom of expression for each child, considering this a learning situation for his parents as well. She may call a parent's attention to a skill or manifestation of independence on the part of the child which the parent will then begin to encourage at home. She sometimes gives to the parent, to take home, age-appropriate materials to help the child develop and, at the same time, to help the parent become aware of some of the growth stages of young children.

She makes a particular effort to plan ahead for days when parents will be bringing in their children with neurological defects, and she tries to have appropriate materials ready for them. This is often quite an eye-opening situation for such parents, who may not have been aware of their children's capabilities or of the ways in which they could help them. The clinic playroom makes possible demonstrations of the ways in which therapeutic procedures can be brought into the home.

The philosophy of the Child Life and Education Department and its concern for families are shared by Dr. L. Clark Hansbarger, chief of Outpatient Pediatrics, a consultant in Maternal and Infant Care, and a staff member of two of the city's satellite clinics. In his triple role inside and outside the hospital, he sees a greater need for relating to hospital patients through their own communities.

"We have enough inpatient beds," Dr. Hansbarger says, "but our patients often live close enough to the hospital here on the west side so that they could be treated at home. I would like to see more short-term care done in the home. It is unrealistic to think in terms of complete care-by-parent in this hospital. The parents often have many problems at home: many of the mothers, for instance, are living apart from their husbands or have never had a husband. If they have no one at home with whom they can share the responsibility, it is doubly hard for them to take on the extended job of supporting the child in the hospital, while at the same time carrying out their role at home."

Like Mrs. Plank, Dr. Hansbarger believes that the problem of total child and family care cannot be solved by adding volunteer services. Rather, he would like to see trained professional teams in operation that would bring medical care to homes where hardship would be involved in bringing the patient to the hospital. He himself now makes house calls at least once a week, sometimes tracing a non-English-speaking family or one which has no telephone, sometimes visiting a newly-arrived migrant family, unused to city services. "If you deal with one family at a time you can learn from the one. Sometimes this is the key to a policy that will make things better for many."

There is not much distrust of the hospital from long-time residents in the area, since they themselves were often patients here. "They rely on us," he says, "which is not the same thing as liking us. Of course there are complaints— families had to wait too long, something wasn't right—but, overall, they tend to use us as the family doctor. We try to deal with any complaints on an individual basis. You see, they feel that we're doing our job so they count on us, and they usually come back when anything goes wrong."

OTHER COMMUNITY INVOLVEMENT

The Hunterdon Medical Center, The Johns Hopkins Hospital, Children's Hospital of Philadelphia's Operation Rebound and its counterpart clinics, and Cleveland Metropolitan General Hospital, in different ways and under various pressures and limitations, are all attempting to find new and better solutions for some of the urgent problems posed by increasing caseloads and the need for better preventive health care. These problems, although they can be most dramatically seen in the crowded ghettos of large cities, are no less present in rural districts. At the University of Kentucky Medical Center, for instance, a traveling clinic, working out of a station wagon, takes medical care into rural districts to patients assembled at regular stops on the route. The hospital also follows up on clinic visits and discharged patients through a team effort with the Visiting Nurses Association. Distrust of strangers and suspicion of what appears to be unwarranted interference, as well as fears of strange medical equipment and procedures, are found in these rural communities as well as in ghettos and give way only gradually to mutual understanding and cooperation.

The tendency of private physicians to move away from crowded ghetto areas and into suburbs and the growth of large central medical centers in cities have led to a situation in which low-income families use clinics and emergency rooms more and more as a substitute for the family physician. The resultant centralization and overcrowding of hospital facilities and the gaps that exist in health care in ghettos are proof of the need for more health professionals and for bringing preventive care to the community.

Less obvious as a recognized problem, but an important factor in preventing recidivism and in educating families, is the perception the community has of the experience of hospitalization. Some hospitals with a very high standard of medical care, and with increasingly attractive housing and services for patients, demonstrate an unspoken distrust for patients and their families which parallels the suspicion shown by indigent, illiterate, or non-English-speaking patients for the hospital. The barriers to understanding are obvious when demonstrated by families: broken clinic appointments, parents who disappear and are difficult to trace when a child has been hospitalized, children who make repeated return visits to the hospital because of improper follow-up care at home, active hostility to the staff or interference with the nursing procedures by parents on the wards, accusations, and even outbursts of temper. Distrust and lack of understanding are less obvious when demonstrated by the hospital: short visiting hours with restrictions, many prohibitive signs on the walls warning of silence and curtailment of activities, purposeful avoidance of greetings and conversations with parents, answering parental questions briefly and uninformatively, if at all. Most subtle of all, but with an unmistakable message for families, is the policy of allowing parents to sit by their children only "if they insist," and to stay overnight "if they ask; if they get written instructions from the doctor; if they're determined to stay." The message conveyed by this last attitude is that a parent is a nuisance and a hindrance to good care, if not actually a hazard, which the hospital—

against the better judgment of the staff—will have to put up with; further, that a parent who stays will not be instructed or helped, but will have to face the experience unsupported. With such resistance, fear, and confusion on the part of many patients and families and with insistence on rules often overriding any sympathetic understanding of human feelings on the part of hospital staff, it is small wonder that social pressures and increased costs have exacerbated difficulties for hospitals and for the patients who use them.

The hospitals which have been discussed are unusual in their realistic appraisal of the needs of those they serve and in their efforts to meet those needs by bringing patients, their families, and their neighbors into active partnership. In perceiving their patients as being in need of understanding as well as technical skills, they are reaching out to discover who the patients and their families are, where they come from, what social and psychological problems contribute to their need for health care, and how the hospital can expand its role into that of good neighbor, then on from this first step toward becoming a realistic force for social change.

These developing trends toward communicating with the neighborhood outside are not always easy to carry out and often seem unrewarding and slow to show positive results. In common with most social and cultural change, they depend on degree of readiness, education for change, and the tireless efforts of dedicated professionals.

These hospitals have made a beginning, using the facilities at hand. They are not the only institutions that are aware that social problems and medical problems are closely linked, and they are not alone in making new moves toward implementing this awareness. But they are innovators and valuable models.

REFERENCES

Cook, F. J. *The Plot against the Patient.* New Jersey: Prentice-Hall, 1967.

Hemmendinger, M. Rx: Admit parents at all times. *Child Study* 34:3-9, 1956-1957.

Pavenstedt, E. A child guidance service in a municipal hospital. *Children* 10:207-212, 1963.

Prugh, D. G., Staub, E. M., Sands, H. H., Kirschbaum, R. M., and Lenihan, E. A. A study of the emotional reactions of children and families to hospitalization and illness. *American Journal of Orthopsychiatry* 23:70-106, 1953.

Solnit, A. J. Hospitalization: Aid to physical and psychological health in childhood. *American Journal of Diseases of Children* 99:155-163, 1960.

Spitz, R. A. The role of ecological factors in emotional development in infancy. *Child Development* 20:145-155, 1949.

Stolz, L. M. Effects of maternal employment on children: Evidence from research. *Child Development* 31:749-782, 1960.

7

Hospitals in Transition

WE have looked at some but by no means all of the hospitals that are dedicated to a new concept of pediatric care. This new multidimensional approach to the patient is growing in many other institutions, often so rapidly that it is difficult to report on it accurately. Two such hospitals are the Herbert C. Moffitt Hospital in San Francisco and the Children's Hospital Medical Center of Boston. A third, the Children's Hospital of Denver, is notable for its neonatal unit, which is unique in several ways.

HERBERT C. MOFFITT HOSPITAL

In many ways, Moffitt Hospital in San Francisco is the prototype of large urban research and teaching hospitals across the country. The complexity of the departments, the interactions between various disciplines, the excellence of equipment and medical care, are all to some degree characteristic of the way in which medical facilities have developed in the United States, with emphasis on expansion of knowledge and techniques and on methods of handling increased caseloads.

When the hospital was opened to patients in 1955, research on the emotional effects of maternal deprivation on children was not widely publicized and few hospitals were concerned with the children's emotional reactions as a factor in illness and health. The Henrietta Egleston Hospital for Children, one of the first in the country to consider the total child during hospitalization, began its policy of parent inclusion when the new building was completed in 1959, four years after Moffitt Hospital opened its doors. The Johns Hopkins Hospital and the University of Colorado Medical Center built their facilities to include parents in the early 1960's. The research of John Bowlby in England had been completed and published in 1951 but was being accepted as valid only slowly and with caution. Policy in most large hospitals at that time (and even in smaller community hospitals with lesser caseloads) was to exclude parents for many reasons, chief among them the fear of outside contagion and reluctance to take seriously children's overt signs of emotional upset. It is not surprising, therefore, that in planning the pediatric facility at Moffitt Hospital, no emphasis was placed on the need to make room for parents. A few beds in private rooms were available for parents who stayed on rare occasions, usually with terminally ill children.

On a hilltop rising 15 stories to overlook the city of San Francisco, the ocean, and the Golden Gate Bridge, the hospital houses the inpatient pediatric units as well as the adult facilities for the University of California Hospitals and Clinics. The pediatric service for acutely ill children, on the sixth floor, is composed of a medical area, a surgical wing, the Special Care Unit, and a Metabolic Research Unit. In addition to the treatment rooms, nursing stations, and service areas, there are a solarium playroom and a roof play yard where a handsome "teen house" serves as a center for adolescents.

A parents' waiting area near the elevators opens onto a roof court, and there is a small interview room nearby, which also serves as a place where parents can retreat for privacy. Smoking is permitted in the waiting area, and parents help themselves to coffee and tea at any time. On the wall a poster invites parents to bring their children who are not patients to the outpatient clinic playroom on the next floor down while they visit their hospitalized child. Notices of parents' meetings are posted, as are listings for housing near the hospital.

The corridors leading from this area are decorated with graphics of multicolored balloons and stylized figures of children playing. Infants and toddlers watch the passing parade from playpens, children and teenagers visit friends in other rooms or the playroom, sometimes foot-propelling an intravenous stand, sometimes in wheelchairs or carts steered by friends, volunteers, parents, nurses, or Foster Grand-parents. Because there are four medical specialty teams, medical rounds create a crowd several times a day.

Most children stay in 4- to 6-bed rooms with glass partitions between room and corridor, and sometimes between beds, to permit viewing in and out and a table and chairs for play and family-style meals. All of the bed units have ceiling-installed brackets for rental television sets, and a fund allows those children whose parents cannot afford the rental to avail themselves of television, a gift of the hospital's auxiliary. In the rooms for younger children there are rocking chairs for parents and Foster Grandparents. Parents are invited to make arrangements to stay near the hospital, usually in one of the guest houses. These are private houses, within walking distance of the hospital, that have been converted into rooms to be rented to families of the patients. In the surgical wing and in the Special Care Unit and the Metabolic Research Unit no provisions are made for parents to sleep beside their children, but when beds or chair-beds are available a parent may set one up for herself in the playroom. A surgical patient may also be moved to the medical corridor as a "boarder" if he no longer needs special surgical care.

The Special Care Unit, which is self-contained with accommodations for 6 beds or cribs, the latest monitoring equipment, and its own stove-sink combination, is cheerfully decorated with mobiles, cartoons on the window shades, and pictures on the walls, all executed by the nursing staff. Rocking chairs are available for parents who make individual arrangements for visiting during the day.

The Metabolic Research Unit is also self-contained, accommodating 6 patients. It has a kitchenette and is the only unit with its own bathroom. Well furnished and with a special nursing staff, this unit has a lively, informal air since many of the children are living here while tests are being completed rather than because they are ill. Parents seldom stay at night here but are welcome to visit as they choose during the day.

In 1955, Moffitt Hospital's visiting hours in pediatrics were limited and rooming in was allowed only in rare instances. Today, open visiting for parents, the Care-through-Parent room, visits from siblings in the waiting area, and parent discussion groups are all part of its policy, and there are many other indications of the changes which have taken place over the years. Two important elements in the ability to make these changes were present from the time the hospital opened: the concern of the staff for meeting the emotional and developmental needs of children and the formation of the Pediatric Unit Advisory Committee (PUAC), an interprofessional committee.

Originally established in 1956 by Dr. William D. Deamer, former chief of pediatrics, PUAC continues to concern itself with problems affecting the patient and his family and makes recommendations for meeting their needs. School of Nursing faculty members encourage activities on pediatric floors that are linked with teaching programs on the effects of illness and hospitalization on child development. This interaction between the School of Nursing and the pediatric unit dates back to 1956, when the first social group worker was hired. Under her direction, a play program was begun as a demonstration project. PUAC was formed to support the play project.

One of the primary purposes of PUAC is facilitating communication and cooperation among the many disciplines of the pediatric service. Membership includes representatives from medical and nursing services, nursing education, social work, dietary staff, playroom and schools staffs, administration, the director of volunteers, and frequently representatives from the Parents' Advisory Council of the outpatient pediatric clinics. When a particular program or policy is under discussion, guests are invited to join PUAC's monthly luncheon discussions. At one meeting, for example, members of the faculty of the California College of Arts and Crafts came to offer plans for redesigning and decorating the pediatric unit, to be executed by their design students as a community project.

At PUAC's monthly luncheon meetings the committee talks over policies and problems in open forum; its broad representation makes possible an exchange of opinions and information on many levels and from many points of view. Although PUAC has no formal authority, its recommendations carry weight since members can, within their own departments, bring issues to action. At one meeting, for instance, the admissions officer was invited to contribute to the discussion on revision of the pediatric admitting procedure. (Previously, children had sometimes waited as long as five hours before being brought to the unit.) When this problem was brought to the attention of the admissions officer and the rest of the group, policy was modified so that children and parents now come directly to the unit, and only after the child is comfortably settled does the parent go back to the admissions office to give the complete information needed for hospital records.

Since 1966 the chairmanship of PUAC has been held by Dr. Peter Cohen, a member of the pediatric staff and director of the Cerebral Palsy Clinic. Under his leadership, preadmission tours for children and families were inaugurated, visiting hours for parents were extended, nurses were encouraged to wear colored uniforms, and the Care-through-Parent Program was established. The most recent contribution toward creating a more homelike atmosphere has been the welcoming of siblings to visit with patients in the playroom. Other projects undertaken by PUAC include planning and financing Christmas and monthly birthday parties with gifts for the children and authorizing and approving brochures in Spanish and English that invite parents to participate in the care of the children.

The committee recommended in 1966 that two Foster Grandparents be employed through the Office of Economic Opportunity program. This led to the hiring of a Foster Grandfather who spoke Spanish (a much-needed skill at Moffitt Hospital) and a Foster Grandmother. Parents at this time were still restricted to limited visiting hours and many families who lived at a distance were able to visit seldom or not at all, so that some children had no dependable continuous relationships with one person. Published research showed that many brief or casual encounters can increase a child's anxiety rather than counteract it, since children exposed to a series of superficial contacts may interpret them as a series of rejections. The question arose as to whether adding Foster Grandparents to a ward already crowded with doctors, nurses, service staff, teachers, students, lab technicians, escorts, and volunteers would be of any benefit to the children. PUAC assigned a researcher to make a study of children under 5 years old currently in the hospital who had no support from their parents. She recorded the time each child spent with an adult companion, exclusive of medical or procedural care. At the end of two weeks, the findings showed that no child under 5 years old averaged more than 20 minutes of such companionship over a 24-hour period, and that this 20 minutes was not in one sustained interaction but often in contacts of only a few minutes at a time. On the basis of the report, PUAC recommended that the number of Foster Grandparents be tripled. The research findings also clearly implied the need for parents to give ongoing support to young children; within a short time, the policy for visiting was changed to permit parents to come at any time.

The Pediatric Unit Advisory Committee has been and continues to be one of the most effective agents for change in the hospital—flexible enough to embrace the viewpoints of many disciplines and concerned with constant evaluation and implementation of worthwhile changes in pediatric care.

Another team effort to facilitate communication and cooperation among the various disciplines in pediatrics is a regular Thursday series of ward management conferences, for which PUAC supplies funds for cookies and coffee. Conducted by the pediatric social workers, these meetings invite everyone connected with the service—aides, licensed vocational nurses, staff nurses, interns, residents, nursing students, teachers, playroom staff, dieticians, and faculty coordinators. When a particular case is being discussed, the attending physician for that patient is invited to contribute. Pediatric Fellows from the Child Study Unit, a mental health program of the University of California Clinics which works with families of children who have emotional and developmental problems, often use role·play to help staff personnel better understand the behavior of patients, parents, and colleagues. With communication techniques such as this, the group members gain insights that lead to better patient care and to greater job satisfaction. At one meeting a new intern asked the nursing staff to call him in when they began an intravenous feeding or carried out a postural drainage. He had never had experience with either of these procedures, and yet he was expected to perform them expertly. Nurses responded sympathetically and helpfully. It is an important function of these sessions to facilitate such communication between disciplines.

In addition to ward management conferences, the pediatric social workers meet weekly with the nursing staff to share information and planning for families being cared for on the unit. Psychiatric consultation is available to them on request.

A new channel for better understanding between professional staff and the families of pediatric patients was established in 1969 in the outpatient clinic of the University of California Medical Center, of which Moffitt Hospital is a part. A twelve-member council of parents whose children are registered in the clinic, the Parents' Advisory Council, meets monthly in a conference room in the building which houses the outpatient clinic, with care provided for their children in the clinic playroom. Because these parents are consultants to staff, they are reimbursed for their time and expenses in return for serving as council members. The council is primarily concerned with commenting on clinic services, evaluating new clinic plans and proposals, and suggesting improvements in patient-care delivery to the clinic staff. It has written its own bylaws and decides its own agenda. Dr. Donald Fink, associate professor of pediatrics, originally proposed the council, encouraged by the fact that some other medical centers had found them successful. "There is no other way to get this kind of information, and we need it," says Dr. Fink. "We can't teach good care unless we practice it."

Several changes have resulted from the suggestions and active interest of the council—a streamlining of procedures so that an entire family can be registered or have its registration renewed at one time; an information center to help parents with insurance forms; a staff-sponsored informal class for parents to discuss health topics chosen by vote of the group; and a food cart, informally known as the "Goodies Wagon," sent to the clinic area daily by the cafeteria to sell sandwiches, soup, and other snacks to waiting patients and their families. Before the cart, families who had not learned to pack a lunch often had waited in the clinic through the lunch period, reluctant to go to the cafeteria for fear of missing an appointment. Another frustrating and time-consuming interval was sometimes spent in billing and payment procedures. The council discussed families' complaints about these procedures, and the payment system was reorganized.

Parents' Advisory Council members sometimes attend

PUAC meetings, again as paid consultants, to offer a parent's viewpoint and to form a link between inpatient and outpatient services. Many children are treated by both departments at different times, so these parents serve as a valuable two-way source of information. One Parents' Advisory Council president, who taught in a small nursery school, invited University of California nursing students to present a "Let's Play Hospital" demonstration for the children and their parents at the school, stocking the doll corner with stethoscopes, nurses' caps, and paper masks. She reported that parents and children responded enthusiastically to this method of allaying some of the fears surrounding trips to doctors and hospitals.

The Care-through-Parent Program

Moffitt Hospital's contribution to the nation's parent-inclusive policies for hospitals is called Care-through-Parent, to dramatize the chain of support that travels from nurse to parent and then to the child. The program is designed to encourage parents of children from 6 months to 5 years old to live in with their children, particularly through times of maximum stress.

With the help and cooperation of the head nurse, Miss Ann Ravara, and the concurrence of Dr. Melvin Grumbach, chairman of the Department of Pediatrics, two members of the graduate faculty in Maternal Child Nursing were appointed coordinators to set up the project. They obtained permission to designate one room on the medical corridor a Care-through-Parent room. The administration authorized a total of 4 rather than 6 cribs for that room, to allow space for parents to live in at no charge. The hospital's auxiliary, with the authority of the nursing service, purchased 4 roll-away beds, and the Metabolic Research Unit staff gave permission for parents to use the bathroom and shower facilities there. The nursing service authorized a salary for the nursing faculty member of the coordinating team to cover one shift a week of staff nursing. This enabled her to keep in close touch with the program and serve as a role model.

Despite the obvious limitations on space and convenience, Dr. Grumbach encouraged the project from its inception. "We can't ask today's toddlers to bear the brunt of our architectural deficiencies. We know they need their parents," he said. "Parents can sleep on deck chairs or in sleeping bags. Our patients and their mothers today don't have to wait for the adequate parental accommodations planned for tomorrow's building."

Not all the staff were equally convinced of the program's value. It took the actual experience of living with parents to modify attitudes. The staff and faculty proponents of the project were confident that parents who were invited to stay and welcomed as partners would offer rewards and gratification to staff who originally doubted the wisdom of the program.

Weekly meetings for parents were begun to provide closer staff-parent communication. Miss Ravara and the faculty coordinators wrote a pamphlet to orient and inform parents about the Care-through-Parent Program. Today, this pamphlet is sent before admission to the parents of children under 5 years old, and copies are available in the admitting office and waiting areas of the hospital. In addition, a large bulletin board opposite the nursing station on the pediatric unit contains information about the program. On this board, parents sign up to reserve beds for overnight stays and get specific instructions for reserving and storing the beds.

Two plans to foster enthusiasm and acceptance of the program among staff nurses were devised and funded by several departments, including administration, the nursing service, the Department of Pediatrics, and the School of Nursing. The first of these projects involved sending staff nurses from each shift to visit the University of Colorado Medical Center. An all-expense-paid, three-day observation visit was arranged, with release time and per diem expenses provided by the nursing service.

Miss Maxine Berlinger, chairman of the University of Colorado's Department of Maternal Child Nursing, coordinated the visit in Denver. "The exchange was good for us," she commented. "We've been at home with parents for so long that we don't always look at our reasons for involving them. The visitors from California allowed us a fresh look at our own policies."

The California nurses interviewed their colleagues to collect questions to be answered in Colorado. Doubts and concerns about the problems of involving parents were aired. The emmissaries took tape recorders and cameras on their visit and, in addition to their observations, sat in on parent meetings and staff meetings, seeking answers to the questions raised at Moffitt. On their return to Moffitt they shared their findings at ward management conferences and with the administrative staff of the hospital.

A second project was the filming of scenes on the unit at Moffitt, with taped comments by parents and staff accompanying the shots. The process of filming and taping as well as the audiovisual aid itself did much to encourage staff discussion and helped to focus interest on the Care-through-Parent Program.

As the program evolved, new needs arose. "I could be more helpful and prepare my child better if I knew what procedures to expect," one parent commented. To answer this need, staff nurses and students collaborated to design a notebook of procedures and suggestions for parents to use as a guide. Eventually, the staff hopes to develop film strips and tape cassettes to orient parents to the living-in program and to prepare children for procedures such as cardiac catheterization.

Mrs. B. and her daughter Lee, two years and ten months old, were the first mother-child couple to utilize the Care-through-Parent Program. They arrived in December 1970 from their home in Southern California and stayed six weeks. Mrs. B. had left her other children, including Lee's twin brother, with her parents in Southern California. The particular radiology equipment needed to treat Lee's blastoma of the left eye was available only at the University of California, San Francisco, Medical Center. Mrs. B. had called the Medical Center to inquire about living with Lee in the hospital and had been told that she would be welcome to pioneer the new Care-through-Parent Program without charge. She was warned that she might be uncomfortable, sharing the hospital room with other children and eventually other parents. Mrs. B. expressed great relief that she would be able to stay, accepting the conditions of inadequate storage space and no privacy, and stayed at the hospital in the room with Lee until the end of the fourth week.

These notes from one of the faculty coordinators indicate some of the problems that arise in a new unit such as this and some ways of dealing with them.

Mr. and Mrs. B. arrived with Lee, who had a retinal blastoma of the left eye. Her right eye had been removed when she was 9 months old, and she had an artificial eye.

After examining Lee, the doctor who met with the parents held out little hope. Lee's life, and not just the sight in the remaining eye, was in danger. She would be treated three times a week in radiology, but the prognosis was not promising. Both parents were tearful. The doctor admonished them not to discuss the medical problem or show their sadness in Lee's presence.

The faculty coordinator (parent advocate) offered to relieve the parents during Lee's nap period, since they had driven all night and were tired and hungry as well as distressed over the doctor's report. After Mr. B. rocked Lee to sleep, the parents went down to the cafeteria. The coordinator, who had made a beginning relationship with Lee, sat by her bed so that she would not awaken among strangers on her first day at the hospital.

Lee slept soundly. Forty-five minutes later, a lab technician came to draw blood. The faculty coordinator suggested that he come back in a few minutes when Lee's parents had returned. To be awakened by having her finger stuck, surrounded by strangers, seemed an unnecessarily frightening first-day experience. The technician left to reappear flanked by several nurses, one of whom was Lee's nurse, who explained that it would be better for Lee to have blood drawn now by this expert technician, since if he left, the work would be done by a less skillful student and might be more painful. Again the faculty coordinator explained that since the parents were available, it would be better to wait until they returned. The technician left without drawing the blood, much to the annoyance of the nurses, who were worried about the routine. Within five minutes the parents returned and the lab was called; the technician returned, assuring the staff that he understood and approved the importance of having the parents present. Lee's nurse instructed the parents to talk with Lee on one side of her crib while the technician worked. The incident went off smoothly, demonstrating to the staff that the technician was willing to join them in giving precedence to a child's feelings over lab routine.

In this instance everyone was rewarded—the technician for his consideration and skill, the parents for their cooperation and assistance, Lee's nurse for her willingness to delay the procedure until the parents returned, Lee for being a cooperative patient, and the coordinator for successfully intervening.

Throughout her stay, Mrs. B. remained well groomed and attractive despite living out of suitcases and having only the public rest room a corridor and a half away for a dressing room. When things got too unsettling for her, she would go out and get her hair done. One of the nurses found this puzzling and upsetting at first. "Here she is discombobulating the whole unit because she's supposed to be so worried about her child, and the first thing she wants to know is where can she get her hair done." Following a staff discussion, this nurse accepted the idea that the one factor Mrs. B. could control in this frightening and stressful situation was her own appearance.

During the first week Mrs. B., who was accustomed to a busy household routine, complained of not having enough to do. "I miss my washer and dryer," she said. She looked forward to more parents coming into the unit and reported her first good night's sleep the night another mother shared a second bed in the room. Her moods varied. Sometimes she expressed cheerfulness and gratitude for the opportunity to stay; at other times she appeared worried and annoyed over real or imagined slights from the staff.

As time wore on, Mrs. B. complained of losing her perspective. She liked to think that her chief reason for staying with Lee was to provide emotional support to her daughter; she could see how much her continual presence meant to Lee. At the same time, Mrs. B. was aware that financially the opportunity to live in at the hospital was a great saving. Insurance, which helped with the cost of Lee's hospitalization, would not cover expenses if the two of them moved into a motel or guest house. When this was suggested at the end of the second week by the doctor handling Lee's case, Mrs. B. panicked. She was frightened of driving through hilly San Francisco, of the unfamiliarity of the city, of the separation from her home and family. The idea of being entirely on her own and responsible for bringing Lee in three times a week for radiology treatments that often resulted in nausea and irritability terrified her. Mrs. B. talked with both the faculty coordinator and the pediatric social worker. "I can't feel good about leaving," she said, "because I know Lee likes having me here. Besides, it costs less, and my husband and I have already had to return our Christmas presents to each other to help finance this hospitalization. At the same time, I feel I'm losing my perspective. I don't always feel I can tell what's best for Lee anymore. I can see that I'm getting worn down and impatient." These sentiments were expressed during the third week of Mrs. B.'s stay, when she was heartily tired of the hospital but still afraid to leave. The social worker interpreted her behavior as indicative of a need to have someone else take the responsibility for her moving out.

Other factors contributed to Mrs. B.'s feeling of insecurity and disorganization. Without the assurance of family, home, and community, she had trouble mobilizing her self-confidence in her own child-rearing common sense. One day a nurse scolded her for being overly indulgent with Lee. That same evening, when Mrs. B. warned Lee: "Settle down for sleep, now, or Mommy's going to leave," the doctor visiting the patient in the next bed admonished her not to threaten her child, who was "only exhibiting the typical reaction of a hospitalized child."

Mrs. B.'s feelings of trust were set back when one night, at about 3:00 A.M., she was rocking Lee, who felt feverish. A nurse came in to take temperatures. She began with a child across the room, although Mrs. B. had asked her to take Lee's temperature first because Lee seemed hot. After the nurse woke the second child without coming to Lee, Mrs. B. said with some asperity, "I wish you'd take Lee's temperature now so that we can start bringing her fever down." The nurse turned her attention to Lee then, and the temperature was indeed quite high. Mrs. B. saw the nurse's reluctance to respond to her request as reprisal on her through her child.

Along with the negative incidents, there were many positive and rewarding times. For example, after the second week of therapy the radiology technician invited Mrs. B. to come into the laboratory and hold Lee's hand while she was being anesthetized. Immediately, Lee's screaming and protests ceased. The good results of Mrs. B.'s assistance in this instance led to an easing of restrictions for other parents.

Mrs. B. felt most at home and responded best when she shared the room with other parents, particularly those somewhat similar in age and educational background. She reacted with greatest weariness when she felt disapproval from the staff. She shed tears of relief and gratitude as she related to the coordinator that a nurse had said, "You're such a help. What would we do without you?" and wept tears of disappointment when she heard that a nurse had complained that she was ungrateful and didn't say thank you when her requests were fulfilled.

During the period between Mrs. B.'s recognition of her need to get away from the hospital and her mobilization of the strength to do so, attempts were made by social workers to help her feel more important. She was given the job of serving coffee to parents in the waiting room, which she accepted without enthusiasm, and had three accidents of spilling and losing things that indicated to her and to the staff that she needed all her energy to support Lee. The experience, while upsetting, did no harm and underlined to Mrs. B. that she needed to get away.

In her fourth week, Mrs. B. and another mother rented a room at the guest house near the hospital. Although Mrs. B. reported to the faculty coordinator that she was being "kicked out," she admitted that her own appraisal of the situation told her that it was no longer right or necessary for her to stay in the Care-through-Parent room. When asked how long she would advise a mother coming in with a child Lee's age to live in, she suggested a week. That was the time it had taken for her and Lee to become comfortable and confident, she said in retrospect.

The treatment having been successful, Lee was discharged, bouncy and healthy, apparently without adverse physical or emotional effects from her hospitalization. During their monthly follow-up visits, Mrs. B. and Lee always came to the pediatric floor for a visit with the nurses, who welcomed the two enthusiastically.

Conclusions on the Experiment

Some of the conclusions drawn by the coordinators from their observations of Lee and Mrs. B. follow.

1. Although the situation was at times exacerbating, it is important to remember that Mrs. B. had arrived in a condition of near-panic, afraid for her child's very life. However, at the time of discharge Lee showed no noticeable trauma and was healthy and very much at ease with the staff and with her mother. She survived the experience well. Her mother reported that Lee's reunion with her siblings,

especially her twin, was a happy one with no carryover of ill effects.

2. Small details can have undue importance for mothers. One case in point is the telephone. Prior to Mrs. B.'s stay, the only place where a parent could receive incoming calls was at the nurses' station, the hub of ward activity. Mrs. B. expressed concern that the nursing staff saw her as an intruder when she talked to her husband and children on the telephone there. The faculty coordinators relayed Mrs. B.'s message to the hospital administrator, who arranged for the telephone company to contribute a pay telephone, on a wheeled cart, that could be plugged into jacks in most of the patients' rooms. The extension for incoming calls had a musical chime so that calls would not be disturbing.

3. Mothers who stay with their children need support in order to sustain themselves and their children over prolonged periods. "I don't mind helping my child. I can see how busy the nurses are, and I'm just sitting here. I just wish someone would show me what to do and how to do it; I'm afraid of doing something wrong." Many mothers, hesitant about taking the nurses' time to ask for clarification or instruction, expressed this complaint. Without reassurance, mothers may begin to doubt their own abilities and become passive or resentful; with positive encouragement, they can often carry out the same care they give at home and learn new procedures. One well-informed mother, who stayed during her child's cardiac catheterization, wrote afterward: "It meant so much to me to be reassured by telephone before coming into the hospital that we were welcome to stay—that someone associated with Moffitt approved of our decision. Then, when I was greeted by that same person, I knew I would have someone to turn to. I felt that I was having some mothering myself."

4. Nurses sometimes overlook the fact that their business-like, efficient, task-oriented behavior is interpreted by mothers as rejecting or disapproving. A nurse complained that one mother, talking to another, was blocking the cupboard where the diapers were kept. Each time the nurse needed to change a baby she had to ask the mother to move. "She never had sense enough to get out of the way, even though we'd been through this routine about fifteen times," the nurse complained. It had not occurred to her to assign the mother the task of passing out diapers or assisting with the diaper changes, so accustomed was the nurse to handling these tasks herself.

5. Parents will always talk to each other, and sometimes this can result in mutual support and helpfulness. A mother and her 3-year-old boy shared the Care-through-Parent room with Mrs. B. and Lee during part of their stay. The boy was to undergo the same surgery that Lee had had as an infant, the removal of an eye, and the mother was greatly reassured to see Lee and to learn that caring for an artificial eye is not difficult, nor is the appearance grotesque. A doctor who overheard the interchange between the two mothers suggested that parents are valuable resources in performing such educational services for each other and perhaps could be recruited to help more frequently.

Parents can also communicate fears and misinformation, however. More than one nurse has called the parents' smoking area the "parent snakepit." Because not all parents are sensitive to the need for discretion, they need verbal reminding. A trained staff member who can listen to complaints and clarify misunderstandings is a real necessity. The Care-through-Parent brochure includes the following paragraph.

You are an important member of the health care team. Your behavior can help your child tolerate the many unpleasant things he must face in the hospital. Your child gets confidence and faith in us partly through your confidence. This makes it very important that you get your concerns and questions taken care of, so that you can support your child. Please share your questions directly with the staff, who can take some kind of action. Naturally parents want to talk with each other. Probably no one understands better than another parent what you are going through, but please, for the sake of your child and the other patients, watch what you say and where you say it. Make your chats with other parents and children supportive rather than destructive.

6. Nurses occasionally wondered if having some parents stay with their children would be unfair to those children whose parents were not with them. Experience showed that the parents' presence had value not only for their own children, but for other toddlers in need of extra amounts of mothering. The staff then began to place children whose parents could not stay with them in the Care-through-Parent room because the living-in parents created a homelike environment. One 2-year-old girl had been hospitalized for more than a month, diagnosed as "failure-to-thrive." Her parents could not stay with her but visited several times a week. Mother's milk was shipped in to try to help this little girl gain weight when various diets and diet supplements were not successful in treating her. She became progressively weaker, was tube-fed, and spent her time lying listlessly in her crib. She was housed in the Care-through-Parent room when Mrs. B. and Lee first came. As other mothers began to use the room, she rallied. She progressed rapidly enough to

make it possible for her to go home for a Christmas visit. On her return, again to the Care-through-Parent room, she sat in the high chair and ate, often fed by one or another of the parents as they fed their own children. She became playful, and after two weeks she was released from the hospital, rosy and gaining weight.

A non-English-speaking Mexican girl patient, in her own mother's absence, alleviated her homesickness by snuggling up to the mothers. She ate her meals at the group table, deriving comfort from their presence despite the language barrier.

Dr. Peter Cohen, in teaching sophomore medical students, makes use of parents who are living in to show how important is the presence of a trusted adult to a 2-year-old. He asks a parent to hold her child on her lap and then shows how smoothly the examination goes. The child is interested and cooperative. He then examines (or attempts to examine) a child of the same age without a mother or a trusted nurse or Foster Grandmother, with frustrating and unsatisfactory results. No lecture is as convincing as this simple demonstration.

7. Nurses as well as parents need cooperation and support when a program such as Care-through-Parent is put into effect. Some nurses spoke of the courage they had to rally in order to enter a room where four or five mothers were sitting together talking; the strong likelihood that the staff was under unflattering discussion made nurses hesitate before opening the door. At times, the nursing staff expressed resentment about having to listen to a series of complaints from parents. In addition to these irritations, some nurses saw the insistence of certain parents on taking over part of their child's care as a denigration of the nurses' ability to understand and care for the needs of the patient. As the

program has become accepted, many early fears have proved unfounded. Irritations have been counterbalanced by rewards. Today, the major responsibility for the living-in project is carried out by the nursing staff, who express pride in the fact that theirs is a living-in pediatric unit.

8. An important part of a living-in program is realistic planning for limiting parental stays so that a parent will not become too fatigued to give the child adequate emotional support. Mrs. B., after a week in the hospital, needed relief, but she had to be helped to make the decision to find a room outside the hospital. Many mothers are grateful and relieved to have respite once they develop trust in the staff, a trust that comes through their observations of the unit. If a mother's stay is based on fear that her child will be neglected or frightened when she is not there to protect him, then her stay is not likely to be reassuring to the child. It is the responsibility of the staff to help parents develop trust so that both the quality and the duration of their stay convey emotional support rather than a feeling of suspicion to their children.

The program is still undergoing evaluation and change. Publicity in the local newspapers and on television has resulted in many requests from parents to live in, and nurses routinely invite parents of children under 5 years old to stay.

Living-in is no longer limited to a single room. The playroom is regularly set up like a dormitory at night, with parents responsible for making up their beds and for storing them away in the morning. "It's like a tribe," as one parent described the project. "Parents decide among themselves who shall sleep where, depending on which child is the most likely to need the parent during the night. Parents help each other learn the ropes."

Moffitt Hospital's experience demonstrates that discomfort and lack of space need not be insurmountable problems nor a reason for excluding parents.

CHILDREN'S HOSPITAL MEDICAL CENTER OF BOSTON

The Children's Hospital Medical Center of Boston, a large complex with activities in more than 20 buildings, is made up of a cooperating group of institutions concerned with the health of children—hospitals, special services, independent research institutions. It is also a nursing school and one of the teaching hospitals of Harvard Medical School. Newer than Moffitt Hospital, it has as yet no structured program for parents living in, although in many ways it is moving toward more outreach to families. The main hospital is composed of a handsome and beautifully decorated 11-story clinic facility, opened in 1967, with computerized scheduling and record-keeping, and the inpatient hospital, in operation since 1949, which has excellent facilities, pleasant decoration, and a charming garden. There is an extensive inpatient Child Activities Program with playrooms on almost every floor.

Within the last two years the visiting hours for parents have been extended and are now 11:30 A.M. to 8:00 P.M. daily, whereas only eleven years ago the visiting hours were limited to one afternoon a week, the change indicating a vastly liberalized policy. However, parents are still not encouraged to come at any time, although permission is easily granted if it is requested by one of the physicians in charge.

The hospital has a caseload estimated at over 10,000 inpatient admissions per year and more than 120,000 visits annually to its more than 50 clinics. Patients come from almost every state and from foreign countries as well, and graduate students come from other countries to learn pediatric specialties. This magnitude of operation has great advantages for the child patient and his family, but it also gives rise to some problems in personalizing their relationship with the hospital staff. To bring new insights to this situation, Dr. T. Berry Brazelton joined the hospital staff in 1968. Currently, several new projects are under way. One of these innovations is the creation of the position of Parent Staff Coordinator, a nurse supervisor who works with parents whose children are scheduled for surgery.

A program of special interest is housed in the House of the Good Samaritan, an older building near the hospital which was, until 1968, a special unit for the treatment of rheumatic fever. It is now a multidisciplinary unit for chronic nonacute, nonsurgical cases. It is, says Dr. Brazelton, "a program in the process of change," and its primary purpose is to use pragmatically, while studying in depth, a multifaceted approach to child care which takes into consideration the social, economic, emotional, and cognitive factors involved with the child's illness. To this end, no patient is admitted here unless a long-term plan for his future after dismissal from the hospital has been worked out and unless a work-up on the child and his environment has been completed by the various services involved in his care—medical, social service, child activities, and so on.

This policy is important both to give a total picture of the child's needs and to assure that the unit does not become merely a convenient place for the housing of long-term patients for whom there seems to be no definite plan. Ward rounds include medical and nursing staff, social worker and child activities worker, psychiatrist, and, when appropriate, a representative of the staff of the outpatient department.

Visiting the Good Samaritan one sees that narrow halls and somewhat inconvenient facilities have been adapted and modified into attractive units with colorful decorations, a schoolroom with books and projects, and a solarium play-room with low tables and many toys. There are mixed ages here, from teenagers to a premature baby in an isolette in a room of his own. There are cribs in one ward, and in another, along with the beds, there are tables for eating and play and racks of washable clothes to wear instead of hospital nightgowns. Children move about; a record player is in use; a nurse is reading aloud to a little girl; a parent is visiting. Visiting hours for parents are worked out on an individual basis, taking into consideration the needs of the particular child, the responsibilities and strengths of the parent, and in some cases the distances the parents would have to travel.

On the multidisciplinary rounds, responsibility for and interactions with the patient and his family are shared. Dr. Brazelton may say, "Why don't we get the mother in here and see how she reacts to taking care of the child and see if she can take some of that responsibility herself? We want her to have a share in her own baby while he's here."

The social worker replies, "She has two other children, and it's hard for her to come in because there isn't anyone who can take over at home . . . "

The Child Activities worker then suggests, "She could bring them in and leave them in the playroom for a while. I could keep them busy right here while she's with the baby, and then she wouldn't worry."

The nurse also has a contribution. "There's no reason that she couldn't do some of the feeding and bathing and so on. Then we could see if she really wants to go on."

Dr. Brazelton then sums up the situation, "All right, let's try it that way. Suggest that she bring the children in with her and see how it goes. And then you can take them on in the playroom. Is that going to complicate anything for you? And we'll give her some reassurance and see how it works out. We want to let her know that it's part of our plan for the child that she should come in. It's not just an invitation—tell her we expect her to come."

In speaking of another patient, the conversation deals largely with the social agencies the parents have used, the attitudes of the parents themselves toward the agencies and the hospital, and the need for their support of the child. Here, the very real medical problem gives way for the moment to a discussion which is seen to be equally important—that of the emotional stability and strength of the patient. "She has to know that her parents approve of her staying here and, in a way, that she has their permission to stay here. Otherwise she can't settle down and begin to get better."

Another recent development involving the medical staff at Children's Hospital has been the formation of a Patient Care Committee, a multidisciplinary administrative committee that meets every two weeks to discuss problems of and plans for implementing new approaches throughout the hospital, similar to the Pediatric Unit Advisory Committee at Moffitt Hospital in San Francisco. While change perforce comes slowly in a large, well-established institution such as this, the committee is initiating more involvement of parents and more understanding of total child care. One hopeful indication seems to be an ever-increasing interest on the part of young residents and interns in such changes.

Another joint effort to give total care to the patient is the inauguration of weekly multidisciplinary ward conferences and rounds directed at discussing the feelings and reactions of the staff in their dealings with children and parents. These conferences and rounds stress the child in his home situation, the effect of hospitalization on him and on his family, and the roles of the professionals in their involvement with parents—how they can be most effective and what understanding they can gain of their own feelings. Called "Patient Care Rounds," they are well attended by all the disciplines: house officers, attending staff, psychiatrists, nurses, nurse practitioners, social service workers, Child Activities workers, nutritionist, and physical therapist.

These Patient Care Rounds, which are the counterpart of the ward management rounds at Moffitt Hospital, have been a major impetus for change at the Children's Hospital Medical Center of Boston. They have advertised and made acceptable and exciting to all the disciplines the importance of the total well-being of the child and his family to illness and recovery. In addition, they have facilitated greater communication between the disciplines and brought new insights into the emotional and developmental factors that must be considered in treating the child.

Informal discussion is the hallmark of such rounds, and Dr. Brazelton is convinced that these opportunities for give-and-take between professionals at all levels, and for recognition of the feelings and particular areas of expertise of individuals, are a most effective agency for change.

The Child Activities staff at the hospital, while its chief concern is in maintaining the emotional well-being of the children through activities and personal contacts in the wards and playrooms, tries to be helpful and supportive to parents in an informal way. It has been instrumental in changing the climate from one of excluding the parents toward one which involves and supports them. Included in their playroom program recently is an arrangement by which mothers may bring siblings of the sick child to a playroom where they are cared for while the mother visits the ward. The insights gained by watching the interactions of siblings can help the Child Activities worker in supporting the mother, and this informal visiting is a way of initiating and maintaining personal contact with the family.

More recently, Child Activities specialists have been inaugurating a program in which some mothers are helped to learn the meaning of play and the ways in which they can play with their children. Emphasis is on the developmental and interactional value of play, and their hope is to help bring about a more mutually helpful and rewarding relationship between the mother and the child which will carry over when the child leaves the hospital.

Adjacent to the hospital's medical buildings is a motel that is unique in this country, the Children's Inn. Built by hospital funding and managed by a commercial motel chain, it was planned specifically to accommodate parents and children who come to the hospital. The pilot project, titled "Partnership-in-Care," was conceived in conjunction with Massachusetts Blue Cross, chiefly for partial inpatient care, that is, when the child no longer requires the constant attention provided in the hospital but still needs the easy availability of services which he could not get at home. There are direct telephone connections from the rooms of the Children's Inn to the hospital, a registered nurse is available to make rounds and to teach parents how to give the care their children need, and a restaurant on the premises is run cafeteria-style at reasonable prices. For patients covered by the Massachusetts Blue Cross Plan and registered at the inn under the auspices of Partnership-in-Care, the daily rate includes the cost of room and board for both the parent and child as well as nursing and related expenses. The cost works out to be less than half the daily rate of the hospital.

Several factors have contributed to slow progress with this plan for parent and child. One is that during the pilot stage only patients covered by Massachusetts Blue Cross are eligible, and out-of-state parents are thereby eliminated from consideration as well as some parents within the state. Another factor is the present limitation of coverage to patients recovering from surgery, although for such a child the plan can shorten the stay in the hospital, release a needed bed in the ward for a child who needs more intensive care while still keeping this patient close to the hospital, and lower the cost to the family. Currently, the Children's Inn would appear to be used more as a place to stay for parents who want to be near their children while they are hospitalized than for the Partnership-in-Care Program; however, since the inn was opened only in 1968, and since there are many complicated financial and medical problems to be worked out for any such new program, the future may bring a more intensive use of the excellent facilities there for carrying out the Partnership-in-Care idea. With its playground area, its pleasant self-service restaurant, and its proximity to shops, bank, and public transportation to the city center, it could become a model for other such accommodations near hospitals to which parents come from great distances.

THE CHILDREN'S HOSPITAL, DENVER: MOTHERING-IN

Both the Herbert C. Moffitt Hospital and the Children's Hospital Medical Center of Boston are implementing changes in several different ways. The Children's Hospital, Denver, Colorado, an extremely attractive building, nicely decorated and landscaped, has done away with limitations on parent visiting but otherwise carries out a policy that is traditional rather than innovative in its attitude toward families. In almost all such conservative hospitals, the unit for premature babies, with its special susceptibility to contagion and need for intensive care, is one of the areas kept most distant and isolated from visitors—even from the mothers in some cases. It is the more remarkable, therefore, to find that at The Children's Hospital the Newborn Center has one of the most liberal and imaginative policies of parent-inclusion in the country.

Dr. Joseph Butterfield, director of the Newborn Center, has even changed the name of the unit. "*Neonatology*, the label that was at the entrance," says Dr. Butterfield, "sounds unfamiliar and strange to parents, so we took it away and replaced it with 'Newborn Center.' " In the same way, he calls the program "Mothering-In." In a unit once used for intensive care, he and his staff have created a setting which at first glance appears more like an informal club than a newborn nursery. The windows have brightly striped curtains, and close to almost every isolette is a low rocking chair with soft cushions. One area, furnished like a living room with a coffee table and comfortable chairs, is separated from the rest of the unit by a glass window, making it possible to look at the babies in their isolettes. This is not to keep fathers and grandparents away, according to Dr. Butterfield, but to reassure them. "Newborns are unfamiliar to a lot of people, who sometimes feel a little safer when they're on the other side of the glass."

A map on the wall showing Colorado and the surrounding states contains pins that give the location of the hometown of each baby housed in the unit. Near the entrance, a large chart lists all the babies presently in the unit by full name, with the birth weight in one column and the daily weight entered in the next. Do the parents worry when the weights are posted if they see that their own child has not gained as much as another, or may even have lost an ounce or two? A mother explains, "You can ask. My baby lost weight for two days, and the nurses explained that they were seeing if she would go on demand feedings; it would be better for her. They told me to talk to my doctor, and they said if she didn't gain in another day they would go back on the scheduled feedings and it would be all right. But she started to gain, and it *was* all right. You can always ask—they tell you."

There are many other ways to find out whatever you want to know in the Newborn Center. The nurses speak their reports into a tape recorder, and the tapes are available in the small sitting room so that other nurses, and any interested parent as well, may listen to them to follow daily progress. The theme that characterizes this world of babies and mothers is, "Everything in the open—no secrets." A mother starts visiting from the time she recovers from the birth and holds her infant as soon as possible. "We've even done it when there were still monitor leads [tubes] on the baby if we could get the rocking chair close enough," the nurses say.

Visiting mothers take reasonable precautions, as they would at home, but do not wear masks. They move about the area familiarly and easily. One mother brought in a small picture of a pig clipped from a magazine with a sign that said "Think Fat," which she taped to her baby's isolette. The sign remained there until the baby began to gain weight steadily, when, to the delight of everyone in the unit, she replaced the sign with a sticker currently being used in a local bank's promotional campaign that read, "Can Do!"

Since all the babies come from obstetric sections of other

hospitals, having been transferred because they are premature or present special problems, many mothers are not able to visit them for several days or perhaps longer. Fathers are always welcomed and often visit daily, sometimes after work in the afternoon or in the evening. They can then see the mother in another hospital and report on the baby's progress. After the mother's recovery, parents frequently come in together.

More than 4,000 babies have been housed in the Newborn Center since its inception over five years ago, and in that time contagion from outside has never been a problem. The staff inclines toward the thought that it is better for a baby to be exposed gradually to the mother's presence than it is to observe rigid isolation at the hospital and then to release the baby to the entirely different atmosphere of the home.

Both staff and mothers are enthusiastic about the educational benefit to the parents of having experience with the newborns before taking them home. The mother, who is often doubtful of her own abilities to care for such a tiny baby, is taught the techniques of holding, feeding, and bathing, and carries them out under supervision until she feels secure. When the baby is discharged she knows that she will be able to care for him with confidence.

Another rewarding aspect of the Newborn Center has been the response from the parents of babies who failed to survive. Since the Newborn Center cares for acutely ill and premature infants, the mortality rate is higher than that of the hospital as a whole. Mothers have often written to Dr. Butterfield of their gratitude that they had been able to see and be near the baby. "At least I felt he was mine," one wrote. "I did all I could, and I was close to him."

Mothering-In is at present a very innovative program that welcomes, educates, and supports parents. Whether its success will influence the overall policies of the hospital remains to be seen. However, the lifting of restrictions on visiting hours for parents throughout the other units preceded the open visiting in the Newborn Center, and this would seem to indicate a changing attitude toward families, at least to some degree.

REFERENCES

Fink, D., Greycloud, M. A., Cohen, M., Malloy, M., and Martin, F. Improving pediatric ambulatory care. *American Journal of Nursing* 69:316-319, 1969.

Goffman, H., Buchman, W., and Schode, G. Parents' emotional response to child's hospitalization. *A.M.A. American Journal of Diseases of Children* 93:629, 1957.

Iorio, J. Parent-Child Relationships: Implications for Nursing. In *Proceedings of the Conference on Parent-Child Relationships and the Role of the Nurse,* Rutgers University, May-June, 1968. Pp. 36-43.

LeMasters, E. E. Parenthood as a Crisis. In H. Parad (Ed.), *Crisis Intervention.* New York: Family Association of America, 1965.

Levy, D. Psychosomatic studies of some aspects of maternal behavior. *Psychosomatic Medicine* 4:223-227, 1942.

MacFarland, M., and Reinhart, J. The development of motherliness. *Children* 6:48-52, 1959.

Merrow, D., and Johnson, B. S. Perceptions of the mother's role with her hospitalized child. *Nursing Research* 17:155-156, 1968.

Moran, P. Parents in pediatrics. *Nursing Forum* 2:24-37, 1963.

Pappenheim, E., and Sweeny, M. Separation anxiety in mother and child. *Psychoanalytic Study of the Child* 7:95-113, 1952.

Pickett, L. The hospital environment for the pediatric surgical patient. *Pediatric Clinics of North America* 16:530-542, 1969.

Ray, Sr. M. C. Role cues and mothers of hospitalized children. *Nursing Research* 16:178-182, 1967.

Skipper, J., Leonard, R., and Rhymes, J. Child, hospitalization, and social interaction: An experimental study of mother's feeling of stress, adaptation and satisfaction. *Medical Care* 6:496-506, 1968.

Smith, S. The psychology of illness. *Nursing Forum* 111:35-47, 1964.

Vernon, D., and Schulman, J. L. Hospitalization as a source of psychological benefit to children. *Pediatrics* 34:694, 1964.

Woodward, J., and Jackson, D. Emotional reactions of burned children and their mothers. *British Journal of Plastic Surgery* 13:316-324, 1961.

Work, H. Making hospitalization easier for children. *Children* 3:83-86, 1956.

8

Small Things
Make the Difference

AS we have seen, some hospitals are planned and structured
to include parents and family participation in child care and
others are in the process of building new facilities which will
make such provisions. Some have simply incorporated into the
facilities at hand the spirit and conviction that families are
important to the best care of the child and their staffs are
concerned with supplying individual needs whenever possible.
Some were so intimately a part of their communities from
their inception that they now have a long tradition of
partnership with families and with the community, while
others are initiating new programs to build or strengthen
communication with those outside their walls.

There are as many ways to humanize the care of the child
and to use the skills of professionals and families as there are
people with conviction and concern. Some of the ways in
which changes begin seem small, almost trivial, but they can
signal to the apprehensive parent and child an unmistakable
message of interest and kindness. Many cost so little that

they are within the reach of almost any institution, and almost all of them seem as simple as ABC. All of them are being used in at least one hospital as a matter of course. Following is a collection of ways that signal to families that hospitals are concerned with human feelings as well as with the curing of illnesses.

ATTITUDES

A nurse gives an account of her night rounds on a unit engaged in intensive research as well as in patient care. "It was quite dark in here, of course, and you can see how close together the cribs are. I felt something on the floor—I almost stepped on it. I turned my flashlight on it, and there was a mother in a sleeping bag between the cribs, with a thermos of coffee beside her for the morning. I hadn't even known she was on the unit, so it's a good thing I didn't step right on her. Wake her up? Oh, no. She seemed quite comfortable, so I warned the other nurses that she was there and not to disturb her. The next day we were able to find a place down the hall where she could sleep and still be near her baby."

A mother at the University of Colorado Medical Center is in the parents' waiting room at nine o'clock in the morning. "I'm waiting for my little girl. Her daddy is helping her into the wheelchair—she'd rather have him do it. Did you see those 4-year-olds having a tricycle race out there? I asked a nurse if it didn't drive her crazy, and do you know what she said? She said maybe it was a little loud if you weren't used to it, but that she was thinking of betting on the redhead because he always wins!"

The director of the Mothering-In Unit at the Children's

Hospital in Denver arranges tours for the ambulance staff who transport premature and critically ill newborns in portable isolettes from other hospitals. They do a wonderful job, he says admiringly, and one day it occurred to him that they never saw what happened to the babies after they arrived. They were very appreciative and deeply interested, especially in seeing their "own" babies, and their lifesaving practices and awareness of their own value are reinforced.

In several hospitals a play area is set aside for well children whose mothers are visiting a hospitalized sibling or who have clinic appointments. The children are happy and occupied while the mother is in another part of the hospital.

These ways of responding to human beings, despite forbidding stone facades or crowded corridors, are all indicative of a point of view, of an attitude.

BOOKS

Children new to Cleveland Metropolitan General Hospital look at a book in which there are pictures of doctors, anesthesiologists, and other personnel in unfamiliar clothing, including gowns and masks. The book is so put together that the child can lift the masks and see that underneath the sometimes frightening mask is the face of a kindly person. A child who is familiar with the book and has discovered the faces for himself is far less apt to fear the real masked faces that will be bending over him. Such a book could be made by any volunteer or any parent.

The admission booklet for New York Hospital-Cornell Medical Center pictures not only the hospital setting, personnel, and activities, but objects that the child will see—such as a thermometer, syringe, bedpan, and chart—each clearly labeled. Two versions of the book are available, one printed in English, the other in Spanish for the reassurance and convenience of New York City's large Spanish-speaking population.

The Children's Hospital of Philadelphia routinely gives an appropriate booklet, *Michael's Heart Test* or *Margaret's Heart Operation,* to the children who will be undergoing cardiac catheterization or surgery (see Chap. 4). The unfamiliar equipment is shown in clear photographs, and the children are encouraged to discuss the book and ask questions.

There are other such genuinely thoughtful books and pamphlets. What characterizes them all is the emphasis on reassurance and help for the child and his parents rather than on acquainting the world at large with the hospital rules. Titles alone can be a clue to the parent. Hunterdon Medical Center's *And Baby Makes Three—Or So* conveys the primary importance of the family. The booklet supplied by The Johns Hopkins Hospital, *You and Your Child at the Children's Center,* addresses the mother personally and sympathetically on almost every page—"Bring with you any books, knitting, crocheting, embroidery, or crewel work that you may like to have to help pass the time." Such booklets convey a personal, hopeful, and reassuring message to the family from its first experience with the hospital.

COFFEE BREAKS AND COFFEEPOTS

Almost every hospital has a coffee shop, so that how and when coffee is available would not seem at first glance to be indicative of policy. However, as with food, the offering of a cup of coffee can often convey a message of warmth and interest.

At The Johns Hopkins Hospital Children's Medical and Surgical Center a volunteer aid brings around a cart every morning to serve coffee to parents in the waiting areas on each floor. Families become more sociable when they have a cup of coffee together; at the very least, they feel that someone is concerned about their long hours of waiting. There is also coffee service in the parents' waiting room opposite the door to surgery. In this room also, a volunteer staffs the telephone and notifies parents as soon as a child is expected out of surgery. Furnished like a pleasant living room with magazines on the table and near enough to surgery so that parents are sure they are not forgotten, this room conveys a message of personal concern.

A similar friendly volunteer service is carried out in the waiting area at the Herbert C. Moffitt Hospital; here parents visit with their ambulatory children or wait for appointments with the staff. On days when San Francisco fog lifts, parents sometimes carry their coffee outside to sit in the sunshine of the roof terrace.

At Hunterdon Medical Center, a small, informal hospital, parents may bring a lunch tray from the coffee shop downstairs and join the child for a meal when his tray arrives. Parents are very aware of the diet limitations for the children and are careful not to make mealtimes a hardship for them. "No dessert," said a mother ordering her lunch in the cafeteria, "I don't want my little girl to see it because she can't have sweets. I'll come down and have dessert while she's taking her nap."

At Mount Sinai Hospital of Cleveland, the social group worker holds regular discussion groups for parents at which coffee and cookies are always served. The very activity of passing around cups and cookies conveys that this is a pleasant and social occasion, not an official or medical one. Mothers sometimes bring their children, who sit on their laps or wander about. Parents' uneasiness and feelings of strangeness are soothed when the group can join in enjoyment of a 2-year-old who has discovered the cookies and makes hopeful forays to get more.

At Children's Hospital of Philadelphia, on the other hand, coffee is not served to parents when they join their children for indoctrination and counseling before tonsillectomies. There is a particular reason for this: the children are allowed nothing by mouth before the scheduled surgery and coffee might therefore seem like a special treat for parents from which they are excluded.

DEVELOPMENT CHARTS

The Children's Hospital Medical Center of Boston has made large, easily read charts showing the developmental levels of children of various ages and the activities and toys most appropriate to each level. These charts are posted in the playrooms to be read by staff members, volunteers, and parents who come in with the children to help them select materials and playthings. One column lists the ages, while the opposite contains a wide variety of appropriate activities, toys, and books—a clue as well to materials available in the playroom that might not be noticed immediately by someone unfamiliar with the room. These charts were made by Child Activities personnel and could as easily be made by volunteers or parents.

EDUCATION

All hospitals educate patients, parents, and staff in positive or negative ways by the constant interactions on many levels. Almost all have educational programs, by arrangement with the public schools, to keep hospitalized children up to grade levels. Almost all have in-service training programs and conferences for staff members as well. However, there is another dimension to education as perceived by those hospitals concerned about the future of the family after discharge of the child patient.

Mr. Lewis Gwynn, Jr., Family Life Coordinator at The Johns Hopkins Hospital, feels that a large part of his work is the two-way job of educating families to trust and use the hospital facilities and educating staff members to be aware of the problems and living conditions of neighborhood families. Education as he sees it is a constantly growing interchange of understanding and awareness.

When Dr. Charles Koch of the Children's Hospital of Philadelphia speaks of "crisis intervention," he makes a clear distinction between crisis and emergency. Crisis, as he defines it, is a change in an ongoing situation, a realignment of forces, and hence an opportunity for new evaluation and growth. Strengthening an entire family through a crisis, helping to make it a learning experience and a forward movement instead of a retreat, is one of his important aims in working with the families of children with leukemia. His attitude and aims are shared by many nurses and doctors, particularly those who work with terminally ill children, in many hospitals. "If we feel that we've helped the family to develop new strengths and capacities for the future," the nurses say, "then we've made a positive contribution, even in a tragic situation."

In an important sense, the difference between those hospitals which emphasize technical proficiency and those which emphasize human values can be defined in terms of the way in which they see education. If education for the staff is perceived almost entirely as a training in skills and efficiency in using equipment, parents and their children learn to distrust and sometimes avoid medical care. If the hospital sees itself as an educational influence that should reach beyond its physical boundaries to influence the community, families learn to use it as a resource, a place where they can learn new ways of dealing with their problems and improving their community.

FATHERS

The traditional role of the father in the household is changing with the new generation. More young fathers are being present at the birth of their babies, actively taking part in their children's care, and visiting in pediatrics, as the fathers taking advantage of the policy at Hunterdon Medical Center demonstrate.

In hospitals where parents live in, fathers have successfully carried out the "mothering" role with their children. Even when the mother is the parent who stays with the child, fathers visit frequently, sometimes accompanied by the child's sister or brother.

Fathers are welcome in the Mothering-In Unit at Children's Hospital, Denver, and have a very special role when the babies are brought there from other hospitals. "I didn't worry," said one mother, "because he always went to see the baby on his way over here, and he could tell me how she was doing." Since there are no limitations on parent visiting at the Mothering-In Unit, fathers can visit at their convenience after work hours. Grandparents may visit as well.

At The Johns Hopkins Hospital instructions for visiting the premature babies' nursery read, *"Other visitors* must be accompanied by *one of the parents"* [italics ours]. This is unusual since in many premature nurseries visits are confined to the mothers only, with other visitors, who are usually grandparents, rarely if ever permitted.

Hospitals with a Foster Grandparent program report that Grandfathers are a very successful way of giving children male companionship. Some child activities staffs are adding men to their personnel in order to give children, particularly those from single-parent families, a masculine figure with whom to identify.

GRAFFITI

A very simple device has been employed at Boston Floating Hospital for Infants and Children as an outlet for the children's feelings and an amusement for parents and visitors. In some rooms large squares of plasterboard are fastened to the walls, repainted whenever the walls are painted. The plasterboard squares are a permanent fixture, and children write and draw on them with felt markers of lively colors, although they also paint and draw in the usual way on sheets of paper, and these art works are pinned up. The squares above the beds are complicated overlays of scribbles and written remarks carried along from patient to patient and have become a sort of ongoing communication. "Harry was here but now he's gone, left his appendix to carry on." "I hate shots." "Mary went home but never mind, her adenoids got left behind." "How come we always have

Jell-O?" "Jane stayed here." "So did Eddie." From a distance, on entering the room, the boards look like paintings by Jackson Pollock, and the bright colors are very effective. Children are delighted to point out some of the less flattering remarks; there seems to be satisfaction in having put oneself on record with a complaint. Written communication in other forms is used in a casual way in the wards, one door being decorated with a sign in youthful handwriting that says severely, "Call me Ben," apparently a protest against any diminutives. This use of graffiti boards, far from bothering the nursing staff by detracting from the hospital atmosphere, pleases and amuses them, and they will call attention to some of the more unusual efforts.

Does it cost anything to do this? No, they say, the walls are routinely painted in any case. Who thought it up? Well, children like to draw and write, and it just seemed to work out. Anyone could do it.

HOME

Taking things home often serves two functions: it is an indication of special friendship and favor, a bond between friends, and it has an educational value. In some hospitals special uses are made of these functions and the results are worth noting.

At the University of Kentucky Medical Center, many of the patients and families served by the Care-by-Parent Unit are semiliterate and come from rural areas difficult to reach. One function of the unit, as described elsewhere, is to educate the parents to take care of the children at home. The Child Care Assistants who work with parents in the unit routinely show them, with the help of a large-sized model thermometer, the technique for taking a child's temperature. After the mother has learned to read the thermometer and has used it under supervision, she is responsible for taking and recording the child's temperature twice a day. She is given a regular thermometer of her own to use in the hospital—it is kept in the bathroom cabinet with the supplies and medications she uses—and when the child is discharged the mother takes the thermometer home with her. This gift has a two-fold meaning: it is a piece of useful equipment she might not be able to afford or think of buying for herself, and it is a sign of friendship. It is also an indication to her that she is capable of keeping her child in good health and that she is encouraged to do so. Before the thermometers were given as gifts there was a good deal of breakage and loss; now that the mothers own them, they take very good care of them.

Another gift the Kentucky mothers sometimes take home is the work they have done with their own hands. The mothers who come from Pike and Harlan counties are used to sewing and quilting for their families and sometimes find that time hangs heavy on their hands in the hospital without a piece of work to keep them occupied. At times, donations have been made to the unit of pieces of yard goods, embroidery thread, and other materials, and on rare occasions the budget for the unit allows for an outlay of similar supplies.

The mothers are always delighted to have a working project—one mother offered to make two dresses for one of the staff who supplied the materials, and the results were a pleasure to both. When quilting pieces were available for a time, many of the women made small, crib-sized quilts that were used in the unit to make the cribs more homelike. But, supplies have run out and now there are no more quilts.

"Why couldn't you sell some quilts and use the money to

keep more supplies coming in?" the Child Care Assistant was asked when she said she would like to get more materials for the mothers to work on.

"The mothers liked those little bitty quilts and I imagine they took most of them home. But that's nice, too. They could have them on their baby's bed, and they were the ones who made them." Her emphasis is unmistakable: the mothers' feelings about what they have made are more important than any financial advantage.

Again at the University of Kentucky Medical Center, illiterate mothers of children such as diabetics are taught the proper foods for their children and those to be avoided. Because a written list would be unintelligible, the mothers are often helped to make scrapbooks with pictures of the foods cut out of donated magazines. When they take the scrapbooks home, the visual reminder is reinforced by the learning that took place when they themselves made the books. Not many hospitals have the illiteracy problems of the Medical Center, but such scrapbooks, with a direct relationship to a particular child or problem, could certainly be made up in other situations. They are more meaningful than gift scrapbooks of assorted pictures, both because they are made by the person directly involved and because they are a permanent possession to take home.

In the outpatient clinic playroom at Cleveland Metropolitan General Hospital, Miss Rice talks with the mothers of neurologically damaged children about suitable playthings. She supplies toys which will further the skills of the children and often gives sample toys to the mothers to take home, with a discussion of how other such playthings can be made. Small boxes, tin cans, egg cartons—many apparently useless or discarded objects—become tools of learning for the child when Miss Rice encourages the mothers to look for his skills and to make materials available to exercise them. "They are often pleased and surprised to see the things that their child can do," she says, "and they're pleased with their own ability to help him." Taking home something the child has enjoyed using in the clinic is another symbol of concern and caring on the part of the hospital.

IDENTITY

"One of the doctors calls it the Bloomingdale syndrome," they say at New York Hospital-Cornell Medical Center. "It's the feeling of vastness, of trying to find your way around in a big place—like shopping in a department store. Everything's there, but you have to look for it, and sometimes it seems as if nobody cares whether you find the right department or not."

To combat the Bloomingdale syndrome and to keep the identity of patients and parents intact in a strange world, many hospitals have initiated simple but effective devices. Both at Dr. Butterfield's Mothering-In Unit at Children's Hospital, Denver, and at the Care-by-Parent Unit at Lexington, Kentucky, there are large wall maps of the areas around the hospital. Families are encouraged to show the staff where they live; in some cases the homes are in remote areas and the families explain the distance from the nearest town and how one gets there. Pins mark the locations on the map, and families sometimes find that they have mutual interests because they come from adjacent areas.

In Denver, the map includes surrounding states, since babies in critical condition sometimes are flown to the hospital from long distances. The staff as well as the families take an interest in the wide geographic range from which the patients come. At the Mothering-In Unit a large chart, easily read from across the room, lists every baby's name with his birth weight in pounds and ounces in a column beside it, and the daily weight, brought up to date each day, posted beside that. A baby is listed by surname only until the family has named him; after that he is "Tommy" to the nurses, and his full name is put on the chart. This identity for the baby is very reassuring to mothers whose babies live in isolettes and may seem more the property of the hospital than of the family.

JEANS AND SWEATSHIRTS

At the University of Colorado Medical Center, before the new pediatric facility was built, teenagers were asked what they would like most to have included in the ward. Their own clothes and a place to keep them turned out to be the most reassuring and desirable feature for most of them. The unit now has a locker beside each bed in which personal clothes and possessions are kept, and the patients are encouraged to wear washable clothing of their own whenever possible. Everything from their own pajamas and bathrobes to sweatshirts and jeans can be seen in the unit. Along with the lockers, every bed is provided with a bulletin board on which to pin cards from home, cartoons from magazines, and the children's own drawings. The longstanding difference of opinion between patients and maintenance staff about what can be put on walls has been solved here. There is also the security of having one's own things in a safe place from which they will not be spirited out of sight.

At Hunterdon Medical Center, a red toy box is provided for

each child so that his special possessions can be kept in one place. Small children are thus reassured that their things, which can be a part of their identity, will not be taken away. The red boxes aid the nurses as well since they help keep clutter from beds and bedside tables.

At New York Hospital-Cornell Medical Center and at The Johns Hopkins Hospital parents are advised, either in the admissions pamphlet or by mimeographed instruction sheets, of the kinds of clothing they should wear while living in and where it can be kept, with clues as to when there will be interruptions during the night and when and where they can dress.

KITCHENS

At the University of Colorado Medical Center a kitchen located between two of the pediatric units is open to parents at any time of the day or night. In the hall near the general pediatric section is a small kitchen with a refrigerator, a large freezer, a counter with a sink, and several units for heating soup, cocoa, and other prepared beverages. The sign on the door reads "Welcome parents of children on pediatric units. This kitchen is available for you to obtain toast, soup, juices, cereal, baby food, etc., for your child. Please check with the nurse in case your child is on a special diet or having tests. This is open twenty-four hours and available for your use. Please feel free to use it." A sign below reads, "Please do not lock this door."

Showing the kitchen, which is a recent addition to the floor, a head nurse talked of the foods available. "We want to get some more highly spiced things in here," she said. "The children who are not on special diets could have enchiladas and chili—many of them come from Spanish-American homes and they like that kind of food better than bland things. It would be just as easy for a mother to heat up a can of chili as a snack for them."

A large refrigerator in the infant unit is labeled, "No form needed for supplementary food from this refrigerator." ("Of course, we have the honor system for Popsicles," a nurse remarks.)

In the Family Participation Unit at Boston Floating Hospital for Infants and Children and in the Care-by-Parent Unit at the University of Kentucky the kitchens where the parents may make themselves tea or coffee at any hour, and where they can find fruit juices and ice cream for the children, become a focus of neighborliness. Parents unfamiliar with the hospital world are at least familiar with kitchens, and as they go through the gestures of finding cups and spoons and washing up, they are reassured by a routine so much like home. At the Kentucky center mothers will sometimes go out to buy supplies and then cook a dinner in the kitchen. One mother was so grateful for the care her child had been given that she came back to the hospital later and cooked a dinner for the other parents and the staff as well and served it in the unit. At Boston Floating Hospital the mothers are supplied with tea, coffee, and toast "all day long," says the director. But they will sometimes bring in other foods so that they can enjoy a dinner together instead of going down to the hospital coffee shop.

A unique approach to meals that is very successful is used in the teenagers' unit at the University of Colorado Medical Center. Instead of the usual dinner trays, a chuck wagon which looks like the ones used on the frontier is wheeled into the unit. The children choose their own foods, often taking orders from their friends who are confined to bed, and help each other. Dinnertime is so successful when the children are given this choice that there are plans to extend the chuck-wagon service to lunchtime, too. The children on limited and special diets are not upset by the freedom of the others, but rather seem to enjoy vicariously the informality of the dinner hour. In the same way, the new teenage center at the Herbert C. Moffitt Hospital serves lunches informally several times a week to ambulatory patients—a welcome change from the unit meals.

LANGUAGES

A slim little booklet, color-keyed for four languages and small enough to carry in a purse or pocket, is supplied to parents (and patients old enough to read easily) on request at the Children's Hospital Medical Center of Boston. The phrases in the booklet are divided into four sections in each language: Nurse to Parents on Admission, Nurse to Parents on Patient Care, Nurse to Child, and Patient to Nurse. Such sentences as, "We will get someone who speaks your language. Please wait here," and (from parent to nurse), "My child does not like this food. May he have a sandwich . . . cereal . . . a hamburger . . .?" are printed in English on one page and in the other language on the facing page; they are numbered so that a parent who might hesitate to say anything at all can find the numbered sentence in his or her language and the nurse can read the duplicate phrase in English. In addition to this attractive booklet, Miss Julie Snow of the Child Activities staff occasionally uses a large cardboard chart on which are some simple often-used phrases. The chart can be propped up by the child's bed or moved about easily; the child can point to a phrase in his own language and the translation is there for the nurse. Although members of the hospital staff who speak other languages are also called in to translate when needed, these phrases can often bridge the communication gap.

At New York Hospital-Cornell Medical Center, in addition to the excellent admissions booklet printed in both Spanish and English versions, the hospital administration inaugurated an in-service Spanish class taught by the Berlitz School of Languages. Funded by the hospital, the class allows one member of each department to attend at no cost, and others who wish to enroll in addition may do so if they pay a nominal fee. A nurse who had finished the course was enthusiastic about it. "We get so many Puerto Rican and Spanish-speaking families, and it was really exciting to see that we could make easy contact with each other. You don't have to have an enormous vocabulary, you know, to make people feel at home and be able to understand what they want."

At Henrietta Egleston Hospital, an ongoing arrangement with Emory University makes it possible for the hospital to call on the language department for help in translating for both patients and nurses. The hospital is located adjacent to the university, so a translator can be called in without much loss of time.

At The Johns Hopkins Hospital a paid staff of hostesses, the Patients' Staff Services, are called in as translators when needed; they also man the information desk and perform many other services: helping, for instance, with shopping, housing information, and even travel reservations. This department keeps a list of its members who are fluent in languages. As well as talking directly to parents or patients in their own language, the staff tries to introduce non-English-speaking parents to others on the floor who speak their particular language so that they can befriend and support each other. This is often very successful.

MEETINGS

Many of the hospitals in this study hold meetings at which parents can discuss particular problems that arise during the hospitalization of their children. The most commonly scheduled are those for specific groups of parents whose children have similar illnesses—for instance, parents of patients with heart disease or leukemia, of premature babies, etc. These meetings are held with medical staff or nursing staff who can explain specific medical problems and educate parents in ways of helping their children. At the Children's Hospital of Philadelphia, for instance, parents meet in the Myelomeningocele Clinic (an outpatient facility) while their children are in therapy, to discuss their feelings and problems. From these meetings several benefits have emerged. Parents not only are helped by the support of others with similar problems, but in some cases have made friendships which continued outside the meetings and led to mutual baby-sitting or visiting. A group of the parents have written an excellent little booklet, illustrated with photographs of children in the clinic and addressed to other families who may be new to the clinic, explaining the medical diagnosis in layman's terms. "The following definitions, approved by our medical advisors, are our own," says the introductory paragraph. The booklet deals with initial emotional adjustments, fathers, care and treatment, school, and even reactions of neighbors and friends and some ways to deal with them. The printing was funded by the National Foundation-March of Dimes, and the booklet is distributed at the clinic.

General parents' meetings are held in many places. A routine meeting held one evening a week for all the parents who live in at The Johns Hopkins Hospital is led by the Living-In Coordinator, who can discuss the available facilities, listen to questions and complaints, and allow parents to air their feelings as well as to get to know each other better. At Henrietta Egleston Hospital there are similar weekly meetings.

At Mount Sinai Hospital of Cleveland, Mrs. Anna Bond, director of the Child Activities Program, holds a weekly afternoon meeting during which staff members are present to answer parents' questions; children sometimes come along with their mothers (see *Coffee*). These meetings are for any parent who is interested, and they are announced in advance and also informally at the time; Mrs. Bond moves through the various units inviting any mothers who would like to come. Such afternoon meetings are also held at the Herbert C. Moffitt Hospital.

At the Boston Floating Hospital Family Participation Unit, a social worker meets regularly with the parents in an informal way. Parents here carry on an almost continuous meeting of their own as well, a family-style interaction which becomes very close and supportive if any emergency arises in the unit. At the Care-by-Parent Unit at the University of Kentucky the director has sometimes called in a family who have had experience with the unit to meet and talk with a family whose child is hospitalized for a similar illness. This often has a reassuring result—the family whose child has been through the experience is able to sympathize with the new family and to explain what will happen and some of the feelings that may trouble them. Here again, there is so much interaction on the unit that informal "meetings" may be taking place at any time.

Open discussion of families' needs and feelings can be held in almost any location and in many different ways, as the diversity in kinds of meetings in these hospitals makes plain. Arranging times of day convenient for a majority of parents and finding a way to invite and to interest them in coming are problems that require much patience and personal involvement on the part of the staff. But the rewards of such meetings, even if they do not seem obvious at first, can take the form of more cooperation from parents, better care and understanding of the child in the hospital and at home later on, and sometimes invaluable suggestions for solving problems. Many staff members in hospitals otherwise widely different have spoken of the value of the parents' suggestions and the new insight they have gained from hearing the parents' point of view.

NEW ROLES FOR PATIENTS

Some of those concerned with supplementary ways of fulfilling the needs of children make use of the potential strengths and skills of other child patients. In several of the hospitals, for instance, children who are scheduled for heart catheterization may be taken to meet children who have recently been through the procedure. This is done carefully, with the permission of the child who is convalescing, one who has been selected because he is optimistic and reassuring. Many children are best helped through their anxieties and acquainted with the procedure by the simple language and understanding of another child.

At Cleveland Metropolitan General Hospital Mrs. Emma Plank has successfully enlisted the help of older children with younger ones, both to give the younger child the kind of informal personalized relationship that he would have at home from a sibling and to give the older child a rewarding interest and the warm response of a smaller child's affection. When a relationship with his peers might be too competitive for a particular child, a friendship with a younger one, who can be helped and encouraged, may give him a sense of worth and usefulness.

At Children's Hospital of Philadelphia Miss Mary Brooks, director of Children's Activities, encourages play activities on the units in which children of varied ages are grouped because she considers the interaction of ages to be valuable for all the children and more interesting and stimulating than selective age-grouped activity.

At the University of Colorado Medical Center the nursing staff entrusts "real" jobs on the unit to some of the children, who take great pride in being a working part of the hospital. Two little girls with identification pins labeling them nurses' helpers carry water pitchers to the bedsides and will not be turned aside from their important job for any minor consideration.

The way in which children help each other with simple understanding and uncomplicated responses was well illustrated in the playroom at the University of Colorado Medical Center. A little boy and girl about 6 years old were stringing yarn through lengths of plastic drinking straws for necklaces. The little boy was recovering from surgery; the girl was scheduled for surgery the following morning.

"They said I would go to sleep, and then when I wake up I will stay in bed for all day," she told the boy in a brisk, competent tone. "But I'm not going to stay in bed because I don't like that. I have a plan. I'm going to get up and walk around and get my suitcase, and then I can go home right away. I have this plan, and that's what it is. That's what I'll do."

The Child Activities worker standing close by made no comment, and the little boy listened carefully. There was a pause and then he turned to the little girl and said gently and thoughtfully, "I think you're going to have to change your plan."

OPEN INFORMATION

At the Mothering-In Unit in The Children's Hospital, Denver, Dr. Joseph Butterfield considers an important part of involving parents to be a policy of complete access to all the information that is available. Parents often become very well informed on the procedures and equipment. In consequence, they are not prey to the fears and worries that arise from questions they dare not ask, and they are also less anxious when they see the medical and nursing staff engaging in unfamiliar or frightening activities. Some parents, fathers in particular, are helped in overcoming their own uncertainties by knowing that they are able to identify the use of equipment or to read a complicated chart. The technical understanding helps with mastery of their feelings.

A mother in the Family Participation Unit at Boston Floating Hospital found that her own feelings of fear and distaste about the procedures used in caring for her infant after a tracheotomy made it hard for her to handle or care for him. With patience and skill, the nurse helped her take part in the procedure by degrees, and eventually the mother was able to carry on a great deal of the baby's care with renewed affection for him and with satisfaction in her own competence. In this unit, as well as in the Kentucky unit and at The Johns Hopkins Hospital, mothers routinely accompany their children to treatment rooms, x-ray, and to the door of surgery. The mother's familiarity with these strange destinations is a reassurance to the child, and she is better able to answer questions and to discuss the child's feelings when she has not relinquished him to a part of the hospital that she has never seen and of which she herself may have fears.

These open-minded policies of freedom to ask, to help, and to be there often build strength and stability in parents that they were unaware of at first. Those who are dedicated to these policies, however, also point out that parents need to be educated and supported along the way and that there are some who need help in withdrawing from an overwhelming situation or disengaging themselves from an overprotectiveness that engulfs the child.

PLAY

Structured and informal play programs and playrooms for outpatients and on wards are almost universal in all hospital pediatric units. We have seen some of the new ways, in addition to their prime function, that these programs are being put to use: as an integrated part of the psychiatric program at Boston Floating Hospital for Infants and Children, as a means of teaching mothers at home and supplying age-adequate playthings at Cleveland Metropolitan General Hospital, as a safe place in which mothers can leave well children while they keep appointments or visit a hospitalized child at the Herbert C. Moffitt Hospital and at the Children's Hospital Medical Center of Boston.

Child activities and play programs are too numerous and too valuable in themselves to be treated adequately in a study such as this. Extensive information in journals as well as in books can be found in almost any library as well as in bookstores. It is sufficient to note here that play programs have often been one of the motivating forces in bringing about better understanding and support of hospitalized children and that they frequently continue to bring new insights into children's needs, often serving as the only counterbalance to an entirely medical atmosphere.

QUESTIONNAIRES

Most of the hospitals described in this study issue questionnaires in which the parents can supply helpful information about the child himself to the medical and nursing staff. Typical questions cover eating and sleeping habits at home, nicknames and names of siblings, toilet habits, and the child's own terms, favorite toys, and so forth. At Henrietta Egleston Hospital the form includes the questions: "Told of this hospital visit? When? What told?" Cleveland Metropolitan General is even more specific: "Does your child know why he is being admitted? What did you tell him? How did he respond to this information?" On this questionnaire also, listed among possible fears that the child may have—which the parent indicates by checking—is "People in white uniforms." Most of the questionnaires are easy to fill in and are returned to the nursing staff at the time of admission. The nurses can make use of the information in many ways—from making the child feel recognized and known by calling him by his nickname and referring to his family at home, to understanding his particular terms for foods, toileting, and his favorite toys. At Children's Hospital of Philadelphia these questionnaires, after they are completed, are clipped with the child's chart to the foot of his bed so that they are readily available to any hospital worker who approaches the child.

In addition to these information questionnaires, a few hospitals have another questionnaire that is given or sent to parents for completion after the child is discharged. These evaluation sheets go directly to the administrator or executive director of the hospital. The parents are asked to check such categories as: "Were you treated as an individual or 'just another case'? Was the nurses' approach to your child cheerful—understanding—friendly—indifferent—abrupt? Was your child's room kept clean?" These questionnaires cover most aspects of care, including meals, admission, the business office, daily care, and so on. Many have a generous space for suggestions from the parent, and the Children's Hospital of Philadelphia has "Please Comment" with several lines under it for several of the questions and a space at the end for "Suggestions, comments, changes, or improvements." The questionnaires are printed in a special form that can be folded and sealed, and they are preaddressed to the hospital so that the filling in and mailing are made as simple as possible for the parent. While not all parents take advantage of these opportunities for closer communication with the staff, many do, frequently taking the opportunity to express appreciation for some particular facet of care.

The questionnaires, like any useful tool, are effective only to the degree that they are used, and the use made of them by the staff as well as the efficiency with which they are supplied to the parent varies from place to place. However, the fact that they have been carefully worked out to stress the individual child and parent and that a real effort has been made to facilitate their return to the hospital indicates an awareness of the importance of communicating with families.

RECREATION FOR PARENTS

Along with providing space for parents, some hospitals take an additional responsibility for helping families of the patients to find ways of making a long and often wearisome stay with the child more tolerable. The Living-In Coordinator at The Johns Hopkins Hospital supplies parents who live in with a remarkably complete map of the main floor of the hospital with particular reference to the most useful areas, from the information desk by the entrance and the cashier to telephones and a post office. Not only is the cafeteria plainly marked, but its hours of service are listed, and the locations of the hospital library, which is available to parents as well as hospital personnel, the swimming pool and tennis courts, and the outside entrances are all shown.

Children's Hospital Medical Center of Boston has a free brochure for visitors which not only informs them about public transportation, but also lists museums, churches, shops, and points of historic interest. The booklet has a map of the Medical Center and its proximity to the Children's Inn, where many families stay, and even shows the location of a convenient parking garage. The public transportation directions are particularly helpful and clear: "Turn right leaving either the Longwood Avenue entrance or Children's Inn and walk to Huntington Avenue. Cross the street to the center strip, cross the tracks and wait for a trolley car. This line will take you . . ." All the information in the booklet is accurate and detailed. The names of clergymen and the hours of church services are listed, as are museum hours, admission charges, and highlights of each one's collection. There are also specific instructions on reaching Logan Airport by public transportation. The final pages have been left blank so that the recipient can make notes of his own.

For reassurance to families who are unfamiliar with the Medical Center and with the city of Boston, and for saving time and patience in answering questions on the part of the information desk staff, the booklet could not be bettered and might well be copied by other large urban hospitals serving out-of-town patients.

SIGNS

Most visitors to any hospital take for granted the presence on the walls of such signs as: "Quiet," "No admittance beyond this point," "Staff only," and the various identifying signs for units, elevators, and so on. These are so much a part of the general scene that they pass almost unnoticed by those familiar with the institution. The photograph of a pretty nurse in her white cap, with a finger to her lips, has replaced the signs severely admonishing "Quiet!" in many hospitals, although the message she conveys is just as prohibitive. The total effect of all these signs on the visitor is usually one of awe and alienation, of being an intruder in a world of new rules, one in which transgressions will do harm and raising one's voice to ask a question will often bring reproving looks. In contrast, some hospitals are using signs and visual aids to bring about another feeling—one of cooperation and of welcome. The signs on the walls of the pediatric unit of the University of Colorado Medical Center that inform parents that wall beds are available without charge and the sign on the open kitchen inviting parents to use it at any time are direct communications to the parents, telling them that they are included in the child's care and have a right to be there.

The maps posted in the University of Kentucky Medical Center Care-by-Parent Unit and in the Newborn Center in The Children's Hospital, Denver, are a visual message that the hospital staff is aware of the world outside the institution walls and that the community and background from which the child comes are important in understanding him. It conveys the message that the individuality of the child and family is recognized.

The graffiti and small personal signs posted by children in the unit at Boston Floating Hospital are noticed by the medical and nursing staff, and such signs as "Call me Ben" on a child's door are taken seriously. The child's name is important; it is part of his identity. In the same way, Dr. Joseph Butterfield's posting of the full names of newborns, with their weights, on the wall of the Newborn Center is an indication of the special identity of each child.

Signs can also indicate a lessening of tension, a reassurance that while the hospital world is an unfamiliar one, it need not necessarily be entirely sterile and businesslike. At the University of Colorado Medical Center the nurses' desks in the pediatric units often have several lighthearted signs easily read by passing children, "It's hotter in Denver than it is in the summertime," and "Due to lack of interest, tomorrow has been cancelled." These, and children's drawings on the walls and windows of the unit as well as the "Everybody over 18 keep out" sign adorning the teenagers' recreation room, give an underlying message to the patient and the parent alike that there is life here and normalcy, joking and friendship, to counterbalance the unavoidable fears and the real physical illnesses.

Children's messages to the world at large, posted where everyone can read them, seem to reassure the children that someone knows what they feel. At the University of Kentucky Medical Center there is a space by each bedroom door in the Care-by-Parent Unit in which a child can post a picture. One such picture, a happily dancing, large-sized Snoopy with a hypodermic needle in the background, was labeled firmly in crayon, "Happiness Is Seeing the Blood-Takers Leave." "I drew that," a child said. "That's what they take blood with. I made that picture myself."

At the Herbert C. Moffitt Hospital in San Francisco, a parent's bulletin board keeps parents of clinic patients informed of services, meetings, and other appropriate data. It further communicates friendliness with other parents and with staff by posting occasional articles or jokes, short suggestions, or book reviews. It is an information service but also a way of making contact with others.

Since wall space is available in any hospital, and since visual communication is so quick and effective a medium, it is not surprising that many hospitals concerned with the total family unit are making more and more use of this means of conveying a message. The surprising fact is that many hospitals still confine themselves in pediatric units to a decoration of nursery rhyme pictures which have little or no meaning and in which the pictured children are not even dressed in modern clothing, or leave walls that could convey so much to parent and child severely blank.

TELEPHONES

At Boston Floating Hospital wall telephones in the pediatric units are placed at a height a child in a wheelchair or a 6- or 7-year-old can easily reach. Families leave small change with the children, who can call home when they feel lonely and talk to siblings, or call "best friends" and find out the news from the neighborhood or school. Some hospitals have portable telephones with jacks which can be used in various locations, and some, such as the University of Colorado Medical Center, have a telephone on a low table in a parent's lounge so that a mother can help a toddler call home. "He's talking to his brother," one such mother said as her 4-year-old firmly gripped the telephone, "and telling about all the goodies he has here." As a device for keeping the child in touch with the family as a unit and as a reassurance that he still has links with his everyday world, the telephone is extremely effective. In a way it can also be helpful in bringing to light information useful to nurses and doctors, as in the case of a little girl who misunderstood what the doctor had said and called her mother in a panic. The mother was able to reassure the child that the doctor would not "tie her down" and was able to acquaint the doctor with the child's fears. He then explained directly to the little girl what he had really meant—that he was arranging for a secure wheelchair so that she could move about more freely in the hospital.

UNIFORMS

There is a trend in many hospitals toward nurses in pediatric units wearing their own daytime clothes instead of white uniforms. Some nurses feel that they are less frightening to small children when not wearing a uniform, often a symbol of hurting or of authority, and that the child sees them as individuals more easily when they are individually dressed. Other nurses feel that the uniform has a real value in indicating someone who can help, someone who has authority and expertise. At the University of Colorado Medical Center, head nurses decide whether or not they should be in uniform, while in each unit the other nurses hold meetings to decide on a group basis whether to make the change to their own dresses. If there is *total* agreement to make the change, an experimental period, with the nurses in their own dresses, follows. At the end of this period another meeting is held to decide whether to make this a permanent policy, and once again the agreement to make the change must be unanimous.

In other hospitals the decision is arrived at in different ways, but always with discussions of how the uniform influences the attitudes of the children and how the nursing staff is perceived. This in itself represents a trend toward a new awareness of nurses as individuals and of the one-to-one relationship between the nurse and the patient. "I feel easier with the children, and I think they see me more as a friend and a person," some nurses say. "I don't see that automatic look of wariness when I walk in, as though they always associated the uniform with someone who would hurt them. They would react to the uniform and never see the person at all."

Miss E. Cleves Rothrock at Children's Hospital of Philadelphia summed up the discussion of uniforms succinctly: "If you're a good nurse, you're still good whether you wear a uniform or street clothes. One girl said to me, 'I worked very hard for a long time to get this uniform—why should I give it up?' But I told her, 'You didn't work hard to get the uniform. You worked hard to be the best nurse you know how to be.' "

VOLUNTEERS

The use of volunteer workers in hospitals is a large and diverse subject in itself. Most volunteer organizations are extremely valuable in the raising of money for special projects, staffing hospital gift shops, wheeling around library carts, and performing the many extra services that relieve the staff of extra burdens and make the patient's stay more pleasant.

The volunteer workers at Henrietta Egleston Hospital for Infants and Children, along with these services, have an additional and valuable, although unusual, function. They serve as substitute mothers for children whose families live far away, much in the same way that the Foster Grandparent program is structured in some large urban hospitals. They provide the child with an ongoing and personal relationship, a special friendship distinct from the nursing care. They often give such friendship to mothers as well, particularly those who are staying in temporary housing near the hospital. Once the volunteer becomes a trusted friend, she will take a mother shopping, help her to become familiar with the surrounding community, baby-sit with the patient in order to give the mother free time, and in general serve as a good neighbor. The emphasis put on the parent as well as the patient by this organization is notable: describing the gift shop, the volunteers say it is a "good browsing spot for disturbed parents," and the Christmas party each year is given "for the children and their parents."

WASHROOMS

The architectural ingenuity of some of the newer hospitals is an indication of what can be done to include families without interfering with medical standards or with sterility and cleanliness. The Johns Hopkins Hospital Children's Medical and Surgical Center is a notable example of built-in comfort that has been thoughtfully designed. The parents' lounges have been discussed elsewhere. On alternate floors there are dressing rooms for the parents, which are used by those who live in. Each room has a large dressing-table shelf with a mirror, good lighting, and hooks for clothes. A tiled shower opens from each, and the hospital supplies towels and washcloths. These rooms are particularly notable for the space in which the parent can bathe and dress in privacy. Since the sleeping arrangements are convertible bed-chairs on the units, this space for dressing is very desirable.

EXACTNESS

A hospital that is well designed and gives excellent care will sometimes be judged by the family on a detail which seems trivial to everyone but the parents and the child patient. Thus, a mother at Children's Hospital of Philadelphia judged the nursing staff by her own standards when she said, "They don't mention things like bed-wetting or mistakes like that." Her own worry about being a good parent and her concern for the acceptance of her child by the staff had been relieved by finding that there was no set standard by which behavior would be judged by strangers.

Concern for these small worries of the child and parent is one of the hallmarks of a hospital seriously interested in outreach to parents. At the University of Kentucky Medical

Center, the diagram of the Care-by-Parent Unit posted in each bathroom shows the room clearly marked in relationship to the unit as a whole. Since the unit is not large and the floor plan quite simple, this would seem to be unnecessary, particularly when Child Care Assistants are available to answer questions. But the staff here is aware that many of the parents from the surrounding rural areas do not communicate easily until they begin to trust those around them. In order to make them feel independent and adequate and to avoid embarrassing them by putting them in the position of having to ask, as much information as possible is available in simplified form. A parent can study the map, orient the room by the X mark, and then, with growing confidence, explore the area at leisure.

Exactness is also reassuring to the hospitalized child when he is given an explanation about his illness or about surgical procedures. At the New York Hospital-Cornell Medical Center and at Cleveland Metropolitan General Hospital and some other hospitals, dolls, drawings, or diagrams are used on which a child or a member of the staff can mark exactly where an incision will be made and on which children can even put bandages. The teaching toys at New York Hospital-Cornell—small models of intravenous units and of mist and oxygen tents—all help to show a child exactly, and in manageable form, what will happen to him and give him a chance to ask specific questions.

Parent counselors indicate with some frequency that one of the most effective ways in which they can reassure fathers about their children's care is by an exact and specific description of the procedures and the equipment to be used. When the fathers are sure that they understand the terms used and the reasons for the treatment, they find it easier to deal with their own feelings. In one hospital an adolescent boy was reassured when the staff treated him in a similar way. The information that he had received about his illness had been given him for the most part by his parents, and he did not trust their explanations. When a staff member discussed the diagnosis seriously with him and detailed the course of the treatment, the boy was much relieved and became very cooperative.

YOUTH BEDS

In the unit for preteen children called "The Dorm," Boston Floating Hospital for Infants and Children has youth beds for the patients. The children here are all ambulatory and live in the unit with great mobility and freedom, playing or eating at a central table, climbing on and off the beds as they would at home. This is the only instance observed in this study of youth beds being used anywhere in a hospital. They may be less convenient for the staff from the point of view of changing linens, but they add an informal and casual note to the atmosphere surrounding the child and indicate by implication that the illness is not frightening or long-lasting. The general impression one gets from watching the children in this unit is that they are reacting the way they would with a slight illness at home, "in bed" but not actually confined to bed.

ZOOS

It is surprising in terms of the stereotyped conception of a hospital to find that some have pets in the unit playrooms and even, in one instance, that an Intensive Care Unit had a guinea pig in a cage. Pets are not listed in hospital brochures and are not given explicit permission anywhere. But as a part of the individual thinking about a specific child, visits from pets, like visits from siblings, are sometimes allowed and often relieve a child of worry or reassure him that his familiar surroundings are still waiting for him in a way that verbal assurances cannot do.

The attitude of responding to a child's fears with reassurance is best summed up by one head pediatrician who said, "Our policy is not to allow siblings under 14 years old. But if it can't be arranged any other way, and the child is confined to bed and really needs to see a younger sibling, then I sometimes tell the mother, 'I don't want to see anyone under 14 on the unit.' I never do see the baby brother. I'm very sure to be far too busy to see who visits. We all just happen to have our heads turned away for a little while."

A family dog who visited one hospital met the patient outside in the playground and went home again without disturbing the routine. The child went back into the unit reinforced in his links with home and reassured that all was well.

Pets on the units, pets from home, a confirmation of life and activity on a different level from the daily hospital atmosphere of illness—will they, one day, be part of the dynamics of convalescence?

REFERENCES

Blumgart, E., and Korsch, B. Pediatric recreation: An approach to meeting the needs of hospitalized children. *Pediatrics* 34:133-136, 1964.

Brooks, M. Constructive play experiences for the hospitalized child. *Journal of Nursery Education* 12:9, 1957.

Buerke, P. Educational programming for the short-term hospitalized child. *Exceptional Children* 32:559-563, 1966.

Gipe, F. M. The nursery school in the hospital. *Nursing Outlook* 3:440, 1955.

Gips, C. D. A study of toys for hospitalized children. *Child Development* 21:149, 1950.

Gould, E. A playroom helps children adjust to a hospital. *Nursing World* 129:14, 1955.

Haas, B. S. *The Hospital Book.* Baltimore: The Johns Street Press.

Harvey, S. *Play in Hospital* (United Kingdom Committee of the World Organization for Early Childhood Education). London: E. T. Heron, 1966.

Heavenrich, R. Viewpoints on children in hospitals. *Hospitals* 37:40-46, 1963.

Hunt, A. D., Jr. An experiment in teamwork. *Child Study* 34 (special issue):9-13, 1956-1957.

Jolly, H. Play and the sick child. *Lancet* 2:1286-1287, 1968.

Kangery, R. H. Children's answers. *American Journal of Nursing* 60:1748, 1960.

Kniest, J. J. The therapeutic value of toys in a training center for handicapped children. *Rehabilitation* 23:2, 1962.

McGovern, A. *The Question and Answer Book about the Human Body.* New York: Random House, 1965.

Rey, H. A. *Curious George Goes to the Hospital.* Boston: Houghton Mifflin, 1966.

Rowland, F. *Let's Go to the Hospital.* New York: G. P. Putnam, 1968.

Sever, J. A. *Johnny Goes to the Hospital.* Boston: Houghton Mifflin, 1953.

Shay, A. *What Happens When You Go to the Hospital.* Chicago: Reilly and Lee, 1969.

Showers, P. *A Drop of Blood.* New York: Thomas Y. Crowell, 1967.

Vinson, P. *Willie Goes to the Hospital.* New York: Macmillan, 1956.

Zim, H. *What's Inside of Me.* New York: William Morrow, 1952.

9

Indications of
Things to Come

CHARACTERISTIC of all the hospitals in this study is the ability to anticipate, accept, and initiate change. While different situations and geographic surroundings make for varied solutions to common problems, these institutions share the belief that better solutions can be found and that the families of pediatric patients have a contribution to make toward finding them.

TEAM APPROACH

One noticeable trend in such hospitals is the use, by the professionals, of a team approach to the patient. Conferences and ward rounds enlist the active participation of all those who can contribute to the child's welfare and to his family's as well. This often means that the parent can draw upon a variety of sources for help. As we have seen, parents learn the specialized care of their children, take home playroom toys that will let them encourage their children's skills, and consult with special parent advisors. In addition, teams of professionals use living-in units for diagnostic purposes and for helping the family as well as the individual patient. Social workers also cooperate closely with the nursing staff and parents on pediatric units.

Restructuring of outpatient clinics is a good example of a team approach taking place in many major hospitals. At New York Hospital-Cornell Medical Center reorganization of an outpatient clinic began with discussion groups for the nursing staff. Staff members were consulted on clinic problems and exchanged views on the kinds of facilities and interaction with families they wanted to initiate. As a result they gave the clinic enthusiastic and imaginative support. The clinic is now geared to a personalized kind of care, much like that of Operation Rebound at Children's Hospital of Philadelphia, with emphasis on each family's having its "own" medical and nursing team.

At the University of Kentucky Medical Center in Lexington, the Child Care Assistant (CCA) became a team member when the Care-by-Parent Unit opened in 1966. The Child Care Assistants, aides who have had experience on various pediatric wards and have shown special interest and ability, have been promoted to a liaison role, educating and supporting the parents who live in. Under supervision and working closely with the nurses who make rounds twice a day, they carry a major responsibility for helping, teaching, and reassuring the mothers. They introduce new parents to the unit, teach them techniques such as taking temperatures, keeping charts, and giving oral medicines, help them understand and carry out the doctor's instructions, listen to their worries and fears, and in general facilitate the smooth functioning of the unit.

Their role is well defined, but they can call upon the nurses for advice and help. In turn, the medical and nursing staffs respect their skills and consult them as team members. "If you want to know what really goes on around here," interns will say, "talk to the CCA—she's the expert on parents."

Child activities and play personnel are taking an increasingly active part in assuring emotional support for both children and their families. The program at Boston Floating Hospital for Infants and Children is particularly noteworthy in this respect; it has a close relationship both with the psychiatric department and with pediatrics. Such programs in other hospitals are moving toward closer interaction as well.

Other team approaches include information exchanges between hospitals: the Herbert C. Moffitt Hospital in San Francisco sent nurses interested in the Care-through-Parent Program to visit the University of Colorado Medical Center. The Parent Staff Coordinator at Children's Hospital Medical Center of Boston had previous training with the coordinator at Children's Hospital of Philadelphia.

NEW APPROACHES TO PARENTS

In addition to these mutually rewarding team efforts, a second new trend is discernible in pediatrics—the non-authoritarian and acceptant approach to parents. "I want them to know that I'm here as a resource for them," social workers say. "I try to meet families informally and tell them that I'm available."

"There's confusion sometimes," said one social worker. "People tend to think that Social Service means charity or interference with their lives. So I make it as clear as I can that if they need me I have ways of helping, but they can choose whether to make use of me or not."

Nurses often offer this same sympathetic listening to and respect for the families of patients. "If we ask whether they can make arrangements to stay, they often come up with a solution to the problem that's better than ours . . ." "We get valuable clues about the child's feelings and development when we just invite the mother to tell us about him."

Children are no longer arbitrarily and routinely separated from their parents. Even some of the more conservative hospitals have extended their visiting hours until, in recent years, open hours for parents are more the rule than the exception. With this change has come a lightening of the atmosphere on the wards, less confusion and crowding of many parents visiting at once, and greater opportunities for parents to adjust to the necessary routine without making excessive demands.

Acceptance of parents has a direct influence on the child's perception of the hospital as well. There are frequent examples in any pediatric ward of a child who was a difficult patient until something he had misunderstood was explained and he was able to express his fears and his feelings.

Questionnaires on which parents can enter the child's home vocabulary and his habits, as well as informal conversations with families at the child's bedside, go far toward clarifying the confusions that arise between the technical and sophisticated world of the hospital and the simpler world of home.

An extension of this acceptance of parents in the hospital setting is a greater trust in the skill of the parent to care for the child at home. This is shown notably by the staff at the University of Kentucky Medical Center, who have taught nonliterate and semiliterate parents to carry out exact nursing procedures when they return with their children to rural communities. Other hospitals are also instructing parents in handling specialized equipment at home, keeping charts, and carrying out many of the daily procedures that once were the exclusive province of the hospital. Parents are prepared by therapists and nurses not only to acquire the needed technical skills but to deal with their own feelings about the child's illness and its impact on the family situation.

"Preparation for hospitalization is an outdated phrase," said one doctor. "The illness, the experience of the hospital, and the opportunities for growth and learning are all part of a process, an ongoing relationship that develops between the child and the adults who care for him. We are all concerned in that process, and we must assure that the parents are included in it and are part of it."

NEW FACILITIES FOR BETTER CARE

A third trend, closely linked to the greater respect for the abilities of parents, is emerging, a trend toward a new conception of the physical facilities necessary for the care of children. Just as more parents are being entrusted with the home care of convalescents or children with chronic and long-term illnesses, so some doctors and administrators are beginning to question the criteria of admission, particularly for children under 5 years old, who suffer most from separation from their parents. The Children's Inn, an adjunct of the Children's Hospital Medical Center of Boston, is an example of the kind of facility which may well be used in the future for keeping families intact while the child is using the resources of the hospital.

One doctor has suggested that nursery schools in the hospitals in which children in need of orthopedic treatment could combine a day of varied activities with necessary therapy might lower the costs of treatment by making it possible for the child to return home at night. "After five o'clock, when the therapy rooms and the labs are closed," he explains, "our service is little more than hotel care anyway. Record-keeping and routine care could be done at home—a far happier solution for the child—and the care that we are equipped to give would be carried out during the day."

Another imaginative innovation, not yet tried, was proposed by a pediatrician. "I would like to see house-parents on some of the large pediatric wards on which parents find it impossible to stay. Perhaps a couple whose own children are grown but who enjoy being with children could provide the kind of atmosphere that is lacking—reading stories, just listening, and most of all, being there in a permanent way, living there so that children could depend on them. It might be possible to set up an apartment at the end of the ward where they could live."

Suggestions for changes in architecture range from motel-style cottages in which a parent and child could live together, with outdoor space for play and with the treatment and diagnostic units in a central core, to units built on a radial plan, with the nurses' desk as the hub, to combine flexibility and privacy with the necessary supervision.

Most of these new proposals are predicated on the growing conviction that children are often unnecessarily subjected to the exigencies of medical procedures without consideration for their emotional health, and that the presence of a parent is the best insurance against this kind of depersonalization.

HOME CARE PROGRAMS

It is thus almost with a sense of shock that one finds that a workable and valuable home care service both for helping families and for the teaching of medical and nursing students was initiated in Boston at the end of the eighteenth century and has, with little recognition of its value, maintained continuous service to the present day. Dr. Hyman Shrand, physician-in-charge of the Home Medical Service today, describes the program:

Originally called the Boston Dispensary, its stated objectives in 1796, the year in which it was inaugurated, were that:

1. The sick, without being pained by a separation from their families, may be attended and relieved in their own homes.
2. The sick can, in this way, be assisted at less expense to the public than in a hospital.
3. Those who have seen better days may be comforted without being humiliated; and all the poor receive the benefits of charity the more refined as it is the more secret.

I do not think that the objectives of a home care program have ever been stated more succinctly. [1]

In 1966 Dr. Shrand joined the Home Medical Service, which is still being maintained by the Tufts-New England Medical Center, to help direct the service and to develop a

---

[1] Shrand, H. A home care program for sick children. *Tufts Medical Alumni Bulletin* 27:32, 1968.

Home Care Program for children. He had previously been director of a highly successful program of home care for sick children, at St. Mary's Hospital in London, that had been initiated primarily to avoid the psychological trauma of hospitalization.

The Home Care Program for children in Boston has close links with Boston Floating Hospital for Infants and Children, also part of the Tufts-New England Medical Center. There is continuity of information and service between the two, with weekly home care team conferences to which specialists from the hospital are invited as the need arises.

It is Dr. Shrand's conviction, documented by his experience in Boston and by the similar London program, that many children need not be hospitalized at all or could be sent home sooner if adequate home care were made available by a doctor willing and trained to do so and a mother willing and taught to do so. ("Too many children are being sent into the hospital for investigation when all that is needed in the hospital is the specimen, not the child.") He believes that much more selectivity should be exercised in the decision to hospitalize a child and that alternative methods of care should be explored before more pediatric facilities are built on traditional lines. Day hospitals, half-way hospitals, extended care facilities, and home care programs are some of the possible ways to assure good care and still reserve hospital beds for those who really need them.

The Home Care Program owes much of its success to the efforts of teams made up of doctor, mother, and nurse, with other professionals such as physiotherapist, social worker, or occupational therapist brought into the team as necessary. Externs on the Home Medical Service, who are the counterpart of interns in a hospital except that their experience is gained during home visits to patients, act under supervision as the prime physicians to the children and their families. Two of the objectives of the program are the teaching of comprehensive medical care and facilitating an awareness of community health needs and resources.

Some of the obvious benefits of such a program include avoiding unnecessary trauma in young children; giving medical students experience with community medicine; teaching and demonstrating care and accident-prevention in homes; finding alternatives to hospital care when there are shortages of beds or nursing staff; and lowering costs to families, particularly those whose children have long-term illnesses.

Few medical centers and hospitals have inaugurated similar programs. Although more than one thousand agencies in the United States are providing care in different degrees for the sick at home, the greatest proportion of these patients are adult, usually the elderly.

One reason why hospitalization is so readily considered and home care is less well known may be the cost to the family. Medicaid and other welfare programs cover the cost of home care for families on welfare or those who can claim welfare aid in emergencies. Medical insurance for many middle-income families, however, covers hospitalization only and cannot be applied to the costs of home care. A few home care plans for children are operative in some states, but coverage differs, and most commercial insurance companies have not developed any home health care policies. This means that a middle-income family might have to pay considerably higher costs to insure good care for a child at home, particularly when there are specialized services involved, than to have the child hospitalized. Massachusetts is one of the few states with any coverage for such families.

Another factor working against the widespread use of such care is that the service depends on cooperation between various agencies and institutions. However, as Dr. Shrand will point out, the basic services needed to set up a successful home care plan are available in most communities—hospitals, Visiting Nurses Associations, insurance organizations such as Blue Cross, and social service and welfare organizations. Just as successful pediatric departments in hospitals make use of many services and hold team conferences to facilitate communication, so a home service could make use of these available skills and resources for a "hospital without walls" in the community itself. One insurance official, asked whether insurance for such care could be made available, answered succinctly, "It will depend very much on public demand."

A third obstacle to home care plans is the disinclination of physicians and surgeons to have their patients at home, since it is more convenient for the staff to have patients housed together and available for ward rounds and teaching. They are sometimes unaware that home care is a valuable teaching tool, the externs on this service having greater responsibility and closer contact with the families and their environment than is possible in the hospital ward. The Tufts Home Care Service for Children schedules weekly rounds for a team of pediatrician, nurse, and social worker, together or independently. An extern accompanies one of these workers, making the rounds teaching sessions as well. Separate visits are scheduled by the appropriate person as needed. Prime requisites for any such program are flexibility and cooperation on the part of the teams and the willingness of everyone involved to adjust to the environmental and social problems of the families and work together without rigidity. The teams who work with Dr. Shrand seem highly motivated, and there are many indications that the externs on the service find it rewarding, just as the interns and residents at the University of Kentucky Medical Center find satisfaction in ongoing relationships with families on the Care-by-Parent Unit. However, a very real problem does exist in that some doctors and medical schools set a high value on medical and surgical specialties and little on holistic medicine. When those in authority are not convinced that "the man who is ill is just as important as the illness of the man," children are often hospitalized for the convenience of the professionals rather than having the professionals use their skills to the best interests of the child.

CONTINUING OBSTACLES TO FAMILY PARTICIPATION IN CARE

These trends toward professional team effort both inside and outside the hospital, the recognition of parents and of nonmedical professionals as valuable members of a cooperative approach to total care, the questioning of traditional taboos and limitations which exclude families from the child's bedside, and the new awareness of the environment and the community as factors in health care are making possible far-reaching and rapid changes in many medical institutions, as we have seen. In others, the progress of change often seems slow and the monolithic structure of many institutions unresponsive. The lack of communication between those who see the need for more humane care and authorities who are unconvinced of the necessity for change seems often to be an insurmountable obstacle.

However, it is apparent that the new concept of care exists and that professionals can no more ignore it than they can return to a world without x-ray or penicillin. In the last twenty years even the most conservative hospitals have brought play programs to their wards, and school programs are taken for granted. Visiting hours, once restricted by the majority of hospitals to an hour or, at the most, two hours once a week, have been gradually extended until daily visiting is routine, and with every year these daily hours have been lengthened for parents until morning and evening visits in addition to the afternoon ones have become acceptable. In the same way, the restrictions on visits from siblings, once never tolerated and then allowed only for those over 16 years old, are now giving way to visits from entire families in areas outside the wards and in many individual cases to bedside visits, even from young siblings.

The mobility of hospitalized children within pediatric units is also becoming more widespread. Confinement to bed is no longer universally enforced simply because the child is hospitalized, and family-style meals with patients gathered around a table, playrooms where children may go and come at will, and toys and play areas in the units themselves are common to most pediatric wards. Even units for premature babies, intensive care units, and treatment rooms are no longer "off limits" areas for parents in some hospitals.

Yet some arguments against family-inclusive care still seem to arise frequently whenever the subject is debated. The most common of these arguments are listed below, along with answers to them.

1. *The presence of parents, whether living in or staying for long intervals during the day, hampers physicians conducting rounds and is an obstacle to the nurse in carrying out her duties.* As we have seen, this argument is subjective. Some physicians find that children are more cooperative during examination and treatment when the parents are present, and many nurses make use of the skills of mothers to facilitate good care.

2. *The presence of some parents with their children works a hardship on those children whose parents cannot be with them, giving them an unnecessary feeling of deprivation.* In the Care-through-Parent room at the Herbert C. Moffitt Hospital, on the other hand, it was found that the presence of any parent was beneficial to those children whose parents could not be with them. An example given was the dramatically beneficial effect on a child diagnosed as "failure-to-thrive."

3. *There is often a greater need for the mother to be at home with the family than for her to be at the sick child's bedside. Families can suffer deprivation from the absence of the mother.* This argument has great validity, particularly in relationship to those families of low income or those in which there are younger siblings. Proponents of family-inclusive care point out in answer that all plans to keep the child's family ties strong must be flexible enough to include the bedside presence of a family member other than the mother, or (as in the case for home care) that ways can often be found to support the mother and child during the illness without removing the child from his home. When the child must be hospitalized and the mother is not able to leave home or works full-time, support for the child can be supplied by a staff sensitive to his needs, as is evident at Cleveland Metropolitan General Hospital.

4. *Care which includes families may not be compatible with smoothly functioning hospital administration and may involve additional cost.* Two living-in units included in this study report costs to be lower for children partially cared for by a family member than for children in a general pediatric ward. Home care costs are less, overall, than hospitalization except that insurance policies are not yet operative for covering them. One of the most family-oriented and innova-

tive pediatric programs in the country, that of the University of Colorado Medical Center, operates without outside endowments and without a volunteer money-raising group and still manages to include parents in every facet of care and to supply, within the budget, many homelike "extras" for the children. "We have an unusually fine administration," says Dr. Henry Silver. "We tell them what we want to do, and they try in every way they can to implement it. They are convinced of the need for this kind of care, and that is the important thing."

Since these and other objections to family-inclusive care still influence some hospital policies and are held by some medical school faculties, hospital administrators, and department heads, it is interesting to note that change has often been given impetus from three sources: nursing staffs or departments, psychiatric workers, and parents. Although some nurses feel that parents usurp their role or come between them and their care of the patient, many, because of their close relationship with the children, are among those most keenly aware of the child's need for emotional support and of the harmful effects of deprivation and loneliness. Nursing departments have been the first in some hospitals to introduce changes in attitude toward parents and to personalize care. Child psychiatrists and psychiatric social workers, because of their concern with the emotional health of patients, are also extremely aware of recent research findings and tend to be at the forefront of new programs for mental health and for total family care. Parents, concerned with their individual children, often insist on staying with them, even when the atmosphere in the pediatric unit is nonwelcoming and borders on hostility. These parents sometimes report later that once they had shown their determination to stay, they were accepted and even helped by the hospital personnel.

A final, and significant, objection to family-inclusive care must be mentioned since it almost invariably arises when any question of restructuring a traditionally oriented unit is discussed. It is a basic attitude found in many forms and phrased in many ways, but what it usually comes down to is that *"the idea is sound, and there is no question that it would be highly desirable, but it is impossible to have such a program here."* Since superficially conclusive proofs in support of this argument can be found in almost any pediatric facility, it is difficult to make a case for the value of meeting the child's needs simply by enumerating those hospitals that, sometimes with far from ideal physical facilities, are successfully carrying out programs of support and education for the child and his family.

A more realistic way of viewing this objection is to consider the primary purpose of hospitalization. It would seem self-evident that children are hospitalized when they are sick in order to bring them back to health and to ensure, if possible, a healthy development in the future. If the research on maternal deprivation is valid, if studies increasingly show that children are harmed by separation from their families at a time when physical illness makes them most susceptible to emotional trauma, can medical professionals afford to ignore these findings? Is the convenience of the physician or surgeon in practicing his subspecialty a more central purpose of pediatrics than the total health of the child? If, on the other hand, the research published since the late 1940's has little validity and there is proof that maternal deprivation, lone-liness, and fears of abandonment and mutilation have minimal or no effect on the child's physical health, it would seem within reason to ask why doctors and hospitals have not made such proof available to parents and others who are concerned with children.

A third possibility remains. If indeed children can be harmed unless their basic needs are met and family ties remain strong, if no proof exists to the contrary, and if many doctors and hospital professionals prefer the best possible care for their patients and favor assuring their emotional health as well as their physical well-being, if, these things being true, the medical and nursing professions find themselves unable to implement programs for the total care of the child, then it might be well to inquire whether these professionals themselves may not be at the mercy of administrators, maintenance staffs, and financial departments, with little jurisdiction over the hospitals originally intended for their use. Parents, educators, and others concerned with the health and well-being of children have seen that family-inclusive programs can be implemented in any hospital, at least to some degree. "It is impossible to have such a program here" is an answer without meaning to them.

While some hospitals still debate the advisability of allowing parents to visit at will, the change to family involvement and outreach into the community has already taken place. Some families are not yet conscious that they have a choice, but others are choosing those maternity hospitals in which fathers have a role in the delivery of the baby and those pediatric wards in which mothers are not excluded from the bedsides of their toddlers and infants. Many are predicating their choice of a physician or surgeon on whether he is sympathetic to their determination to be near their children.

As with all changes, the new dimensions of family-inclusive hospital care and the possibilities of part-time hospitals, home care, and living-in facilities give rise to new problems and often to some periods of stress or confusion. Parents, particularly in times of worry and tension, are not always reasonable and cooperative. Nurses and doctors with great responsibilities and with busy schedules and difficult decisions to make are not always the calm and superhuman healers that the public would like to think them; beds and equipment are sometimes in short supply and administrative, financial, and maintenance departments have problems of their own.

Nevertheless, as the hospitals in this study have shown, pediatric care has changed since yesterday and will continue to change tomorrow. The rapidity with which this change comes about will depend to a great degree on public demand. As parents become more aware of their responsibility for protecting their children from emotional damage, they will, as consumers, shop carefully for hospitals which will meet their standards and for insurance which makes home care possible. As the evidence grows that new dimensions in care are needed for the safety of tomorrow's children, concerned doctors and nurses and the schools that train them will teach greater understanding of the social, economic, and environmental factors in pediatrics.

Together, parents and professionals are reemphasizing human values in the hospital care of children, moving from the concepts of isolation, sterility, and silence to ask, with new meaning, T. S. Eliot's questions:

Where is the Life we have lost in living?
Where is the wisdom we have lost in knowledge?
Where is the knowledge we have lost in information?[2]

---

[2]From "Choruses from 'The Rock,' " in *Collected Poems 1909-1962*, by T. S. Eliot. By permission of the publishers, Harcourt Brace Jovanovich, Inc.

REFERENCES

Barnett, C. R., Leiderman, P. H., and Grobstein, R.   Neonatal separation: The maternal side of interactional deprivation. *Pediatrics* 45:197-205, 1970.

Brown, E. L. *Newer Dimensions of Patient Care.* New York: Russell Sage Foundation, 1961.

Caplan, G. *Concepts of Mental Health and Consultation* (Children's Bureau Publication No. 373). Washington, D.C.: Government Printing Office, 1959.

Great Britain Platt Committee. *The Welfare of Children in Hospital.* London: Her Majesty's Stationery Office, 1959.

Green, M. Integration of ambulatory services in a children's hospital: A unifying design. *American Journal of Diseases of Children* 110:178-184, 1965.

Jackson, E. B., et al. A hospital rooming-in unit for four newborn infants and their mothers. *Pediatrics* 1:28-43, 1948.

Klein, D. C., and Lindemann, E.   Preventive Intervention in Individual and Family Crisis Situations. In G. Caplan (Ed.), *Prevention of Mental Disorders in Children.* New York: Basic Books, 1961.

Nuffield Foundation. *Children in Hospital: Studies in Planning.* New York: Oxford University Press, 1963.

Shrand, H. Home care scheme for sick children. *Nursing Times* 60:1113, 1964.

Shrand, H. Behavior change in sick children nursed at home. *Pediatrics* 36:604-607, 1965.

Silver, H. K., et al. A program to increase health care for children: The Pediatric Nurse Practitioner Program. *Pediatrics* 39:756-760, 1967.

Solnit, A. J. Hospitalization: Aid to physical and psychological health in childhood. *American Journal of Diseases of Children* 99:155-163, 1960.

Spock, B., and Lerrigo, M. C. *Caring for Your Disabled Child.* New York: Macmillan, 1965.

Watkins, A. G., and Lewis-Fanning, E. Incidence of cross-infection in children's wards. *British Medical Journal* 2:616-619, 1949.

Index